DATE DUE

OCT 2	1980	JAN 3 0	1981
OCT 6	1980		
		APR 1 6	1981
OCT 1 3	1980	APR 2 3	1981
NOV 3	1980	NOV 9	1981
		NOV 3 0	1981
DEC 2 2	1980	JAN 7	1981
JAN 5	1981	FEB 1 7	1982
		MAR 4	1982
JAN 2 2	1981	MAR 1 8	1982

inside
football

mike conklin

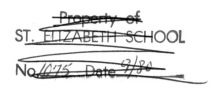

Contemporary Books, Inc.
Chicago

Library of Congress Cataloging in Publication Data

Conklin, Mike.
    Inside football.

    Includes index.
    1. Football.   I. Title.
GV951.C636   1978   796.33'2'0973   78-57466
ISBN 0-8092-7586-4
ISBN 0-8092-7585-6 pbk.

Published by Contemporary Books, Inc.
180 North Michigan Avenue, Chicago, Illinois 60601
Manufactured in the United States of America
Library of Congress Catalog Card Number: 78-57466
International Standard Book Number: 0-8092-7586-4 (cloth)
                                    0-8092-7585-6 (paper)

Published simultaneously in Canada by
Beaverbooks
953 Dillingham Road
Pickering, Ontario L1W 1Z7
Canada

contents

preface

It would be difficult to imagine a sport more revered in this country than football. From September to January, it holds a grip on Americans that is spellbinding.

The National Football League's season-ending Super Bowl always attracts one of television's largest audiences of the year. Annual attendance at regular season professional games is pushing the 15-million mark.

But that's really just the tip of the iceberg. Football reaches into every corner of the country with games being played at the college, high school, junior high, and kids league levels.

One way or another, football touches everyone's life. Whether you're one of the 35-million who attends a college game, one of the millions more who go to a high school game, or one of the millions who has played it, the sport has left some sort of an impression on you.

Family reunions are organized around viewing of important games. Marriages have been known to go on the rocks because of doting husbands who have spent one too many afternoons in front of the television set watching their favorite team. Hard-to-get tickets are bequeathed to friends and relatives. Presidents have lost votes for backing the "wrong" teams.

The entire Army and Navy pause each year to watch one game.

Football has a uniquely American flavor. It was born in this country, nurtured here, and has grown into our most popular pastime. The sport embodies just about everything this nation is: It's hard-hitting, fast, full of action, rugged, full of teamwork, innovative, colorful, and original.

It is also a sport that is complex to some, simple to others. I have attempted to reach a middle ground in this book. There's something for everyone: the coach, player, and spectator. My purpose is to give insights on fundamentals and techniques in easy-to-read fashion. But I also have attempted to give a little more. Hopefully I've succeeded.

In putting this book together, I owe a special debt of thanks to Sharon Petty, who illustrated much of my writing with her photography; Tom Beck and his Elmhurst College football team, who posed for many of the pictures; the *Chicago Tribune;* Doug Bean, who helped me with some of the research; Diane Conklin, a diligent typer; and the sports information offices at the University of Illinois, Michigan, Purdue, Notre Dame, Arkansas, Indiana State, Northern Illinois, Penn State, and Texas for their contributions.

—Mike Conklin

CAPACITY CROWDS ARE commonplace on Saturday afternoons during the college season or Sunday afternoons for the pros, even when the stadiums are as large as Michigan's 101,701-seat facility in Ann Arbor.

chapter 1
FOOTBALL: YESTERDAY TO TODAY

"I had pro offers from the Detroit Lions and the Green Bay Packers, who were pretty hard up for linemen in those days. If I had gone into professional football my name might have been a household word today."—Gerald Ford, Feb. 3, 1974

Man has been kicking a ball around for centuries, but the traditional birth date for football in the United States is Nov. 6, 1869, in New Brunswick, N.J., when Princeton and Rutgers teams gathered for the first game. Essentially soccer, the contest that was played that afternoon bore little resemblance to the sport as we now know it. There were 25 men to a side, no uniforms, a few spectators, and the final score was 6–4 in favor of Rutgers.

The second Harvard-Yale game of 1875 is a better candidate for the ancestor of modern football, for it combined soccer (kicking) and rugby (running). Still it would be nearly half a century before a football game was played that would be recognizable to today's fan.

The annual renewal of that game and subsequent addition of such other playing schools as Yale, Wesleyan, Navy, Army, Cornell, Harvard, and Penn served as the cradle for football in this country.

EARLY DAYS

The most influential and important person in those early years was Walter Camp, an all-around Yale athlete who was responsible for introducing a number of modifications of British Rugby Union rules that were then the basic framework for the sport. Camp's innovating gave the game its unique American character.

First, Camp pioneered the notion that the schools interested in playing this new sport get together to form the American Football Rules Committee. This organization later merged in 1906 with Army Capt. Palmer E. Pierce's Intercollegiate Athletic Association and became known

1

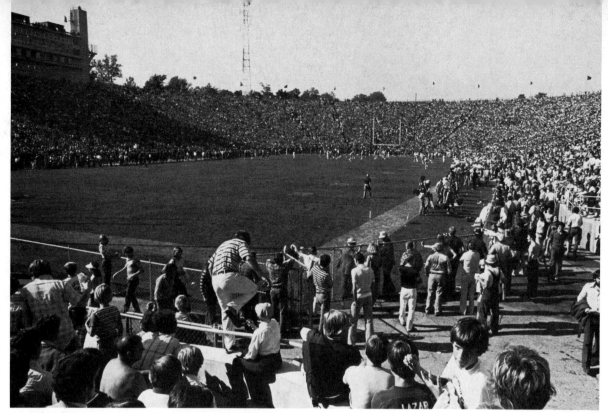

A VIEW FROM the stands in Purdue's Ross-Ade Stadium.

as the National Collegiate Athletic Association in 1910.

Before that, Camp was responsible for introducing such refinements as the scrimmage line and a series of downs to make it different from rugby.

Soon came other changes such as the center snap, reduction of the number of players on a team from 15 to 11 with 7 in the line and 4 in the backfield, a regulation-sized field, and uniform scoring. The first point system, which later was changed, consisted of: 1 point for a safety, 2 for a touchdown, 4 for a goal following a touchdown, and 5 for a field goal.

In 1888, Camp introduced tackling below the waist, which paved the way for close-order formations before the snap in contrast to such early gimmicks as the flying wedge, tandems, turtle backs, and boxes for offensive alignments.

Eventually, Camp and other pioneers got down to such items as eligibility, and in 1895 it was ruled that only undergraduate students could represent their colleges.

Football in those early days was more a participant sport than a spectator sport. After the turn of the century with the introduction of such popular institutions as bowl games, All-American selections, conferences, and inter-regional competition, the number of spectators increased.

Additionally, the exploits of such early heroes as Jim Thorpe, Pete Henry, Ernie Nevers, Red Grange, Amos Alonzo Stagg, Knute Rockne, and Walter Eckersall whetted the public's appetite and gave the sport an immense boost.

Before long, huge stadiums were sprouting all over the country to accommodate the growing interest in this new game. The growth of football dynasties at such schools as Notre Dame, Fordham, Stanford, University of Chicago, and the service academies did even more to generate enthusiasm.

PROFESSIONAL BEGINNINGS

But it was the early desire to play that also served as the springboard for professional football. The seeds were first

THE CROWDS MAY not be as large for small-college and high-school games, but usually they're just as enthusiastic.

planted by the numerous amateur football clubs which flourished in the 1890s—mainly in Pennsylvania. Many of the players learned the sport in college or as spectators at some of those early amateur games.

In 1895 the first person known to have been paid to play football, sixteen-year-old John Brallier, a high school phenom, suited up against Jeannette, Pa. He was paid $10 by the YMCA in Latrobe, Pa. It must have worked. Latrobe won 12–0.

Following Latrobe's lead, many football clubs started paying players. Some college athletes competed both for their schools and clubs since there were no rules then to prohibit the practice. In addition, professional baseball clubs sponsored football teams, and players and coaches such as Christy Mathewson and Connie Mack were among those to make their mark in both activities.

Most of the early professional football action took place in Pennsylvania, but it soon spread to Ohio and upstate New York at the start of the 20th Century.

Among the early powerhouses were the Canton Bulldogs and Massillon Tigers in Ohio.

Salaries for players rose as clubs tried to outbid each other for the better players. Some athletes received as much as $200 per game as attendance approached 10,000. Not even a bribe scandal in 1906 involving a Canton coach and player could dim interest in the sport.

One of the big breakthroughs for professional football occurred in 1918, when the Great Lakes Naval Training Station just outside Chicago put together a team of college all-stars that won the Rose Bowl game from a similar service team from the Mare Island, California, naval base. It was significant because it drew much national attention and helped spark the idea of putting together teams with big-name college players for the purpose of increasing crowds.

Birth of the NFL

In 1920 came the first real attempt to form a professional league, the forerunner

THE MICHIGAN MARCHING band's routines are as precise as those of the Wolverine football team.

PURDUE'S BAND GETS ready to take the field for a halftime show.

THE EXPLOITS OF the football players aren't the only attractions during football games.

of the present-day National Football League, which traces its roots to 1920 when pioneers George Halas of Chicago and Ralph Hay of Canton, Ohio, gathered in an auto showroom in Canton Sept. 17 with representatives of nine other teams to lay the groundwork for the American Professional Football Association.

The first season was a casual affair. Two of the nine clubs disbanded before they started playing games. The charter members were the Canton Bulldogs, Massillon Tigers, Akron Pros, Dayton Triangles, Cleveland Indians, Rochester Jeffersons, Rock Island Independents, Muncie Tigers, Hammond Pros, Chicago Cardinals, and Decatur Staleys. Before the first season could get underway, though, Massillon and Muncie dropped out and were replaced by the Chicago Tigers, Detroit Heralds, Buffalo All-Americans, and Co-lumbus Panhandles.

The Decatur Staleys were sponsored by a starch company and the Detroit Heralds by a newspaper. Many of the teams were sponsored by local companies.

Jim Thorpe, probably the most popular athlete of his day, was the professional league's first president, a move calculated to give the group more recognition. Thorpe held the job only a year before he was replaced by Joe Carr, who held the position until his death in 1939. Elmer Layden was the next league boss followed by Bert Bell, and Pete Rozelle, today's commissioner. George Halas, owner of the Chicago Bears, is the only survivor of that original league.

The early years of the league were marked by many franchise moves as owners generally were drawn to the larger cities, where bigger attendance and thus more revenue were available.

PROFESSIONAL FOOTBALL COMES OF AGE

The league's first big year was 1925, when Chicago Bears owner George Halas, a league pioneer who had moved his team from Decatur, persuaded Illinois All-American Red Grange to join his team. Grange was the most famous college player of the day and Halas immediately took his Bears on a barnstorming tour.

Halas' signing of Grange gave the fledgling league credibility in the eyes of the general football public. The price tag for the flashy running back was a princely $50,000, but the publicity and profits gained from the transaction and subsequent tour made it a bargain.

Grange soon was followed into professional football by such other famous college stars as Bronko Nagurski, Ernie Nevers, Don Hutson, and Dutch Clark, and the National Football League was on its way.

Halas, Washington's George Preston Marshall, and Green Bay's Curly Lambeau, among others, helped things along by altering a few rules to create more excitement. The goal posts were moved to the goal lines to help increase extra point and field goal scoring, passing was encouraged, hash marks were introduced, a college draft of seniors was established, and the 1932 championship game was even moved indoors to the Chicago Stadium because of bad weather.

Like the league itself, the determining of champions in the NFL has seen much change. Originally, the winner simply was the team with the best overall record at the conclusion of the season. When the NFL became large enough for divisions in 1933, however, the championship was decided by a playoff between divisional winners.

The wide-open approach got a bigger boost when such passers as Sammy Baugh and Arnie Herber joined the league and there were targets such as Hutson to make the catches.

EXPANSION

Attendance declined during the Depression and war years. In 1946, there was the added problem of an expansion league: The All-American Football Conference (AAFC). When it folded in 1950, three of its teams, the Baltimore Colts, San Francisco 49ers, and Cleveland Browns, were absorbed into the NFL.

Professional football prospered as never before in the 1950s with television helping it to gain even more exposure. Federal Judge Allan K. Grim upheld the concept of blacking out home football games on TV, and this ruling helped immensely in filling local stadiums because games couldn't be seen for free by hometown fans. The league signed its first national TV contract with CBS in 1956.

Another expansion league, the American Football League, was founded in 1960, and its credibility quickly grew with the signing of several top college stars including Joe Namath. The AFL also won many fans with an even more wide-open brand of ball in a number of cities new to pro football such as San Diego, Houston, Denver, and Kansas City.

MERGER

With the merger of the NFL and the AFL, starting with the 1966 season, the Super Bowl, as we know it today, was inaugurated January 15, 1967. The Green Bay Packers of the older league were an easy 35-10 winner over the Kansas City Chiefs before 61,946 fans in Los Angeles. The National Conference teams dominated the early games, but the American Conference teams rolled in the 1970s until Dallas beat Denver 27-10 in the 1978 Super Bowl XII before 76,400 spectators.

SOME IOWA MUSICIANS tune up on the sidelines.

THESE CHEERLEADERS celebrate a touchdown.

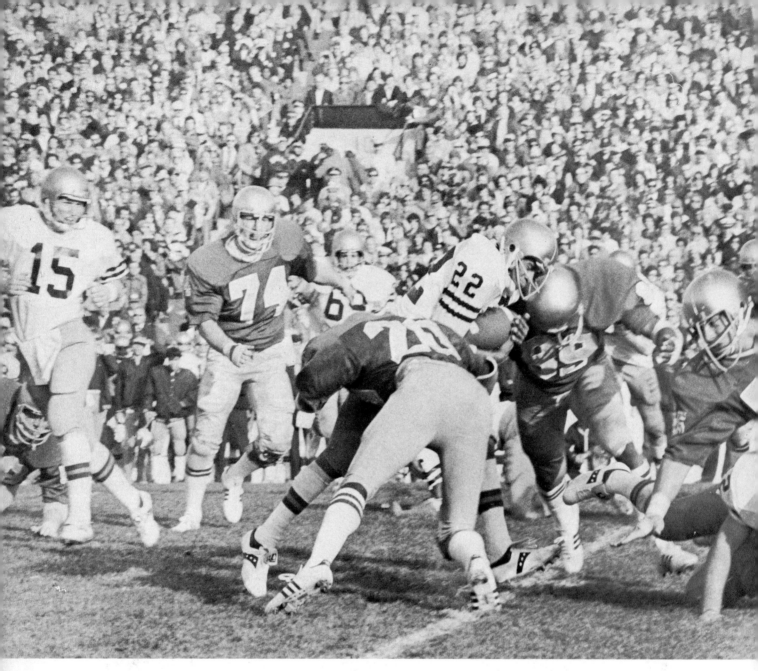

NOTRE DAME AND Navy mix it up on the football field.

The current playoffs are organized so that a representative from the AFC and the NFC meet in the Super Bowl. Each conference has its own four-team playoff to determine that team.

The conference playoff fields are comprised of all the division champions and a wild-card team, the club in each conference with the best record that didn't win a divisional title.

LEAGUE ORGANIZATION

Here is the current lineup of the NFL:

AFC

Eastern Division—Baltimore Colts, Buffalo Bills, Miami Dolphins, New England Patriots, and New York Jets.

Central Division—Cincinnati Bengals, Cleveland Browns, Houston Oilers, and Pittsburgh Steelers.

Western Division—Denver Broncos, Kansas City Chiefs, Oakland Raiders, San Diego Chargers, and Seattle Seahawks.

FOOTBALL GAMES ARE a chance for friends to gather for a pre-game tailgate party.

SOME OF THE tailgate parties are fancier than others.

TEXAS AND SOUTHERN Methodist are old rivals on the football field.

NFC

Eastern Division—Dallas Cowboys, New York Giants, Philadelphia Eagles, St. Louis Cardinals, and Washington Redskins.

Central Division—Chicago Bears, Detroit Lions, Green Bay Packers, Minnesota Vikings, and Tampa Bay Buccaneers.

Western Division—Atlanta Falcons, Los Angeles Rams, New Orleans Saints, and San Francisco 49ers.

In addition to the NFL, there is the Canadian Football League (CFL) with teams in Ottawa, Hamilton, Montreal, Toronto, Saskatchewan, Winnipeg, Edmonton, British Columbia, and Calgary. The rules are different and the game is more wide-open with a larger field and only three downs to get a first down.

There also are numerous minor professional leagues in the United States such as the Northern States League, Eastern League, and Midwest League. The make-up of these leagues undergoes change almost annually with shifting and folding of franchises—usually brought on by financial problems.

COLLEGE ORGANIZATION

Football in the college ranks can be more difficult to follow because there are several levels of competition and separate governing bodies.

Almost all collegiate teams belong to either the National Collegiate Athletic Association (NCAA) or the National Association of Intercollegiate Athletics (NAIA). The junior colleges, or two-year schools, usually are aligned with the National Junior College Athletic Association (NJCAA).

There are just under 500 NCAA schools with football teams. Of this number, approximately 145 are classified as Division I, which commonly is referred to as the major college level. This division, as a result of 1978 NCAA legislation, is subdivided further into 1-A and 1-AA levels based on newly established guidelines based on average attendance, stadium size, and number of sports offered by the respective institutions.

Many NCAA schools have aligned themselves with other schools to comprise conferences based on regional considerations. The best-known conferences and their members are:

Atlantic Coast—Clemson, Duke, Maryland, North Carolina, North Carolina State, Virginia, and Wake Forest.

Big Eight—Colorado, Iowa State, Kansas, Kansas State, Missouri, Nebraska, Oklahoma, and Oklahoma State.

Big Ten—Illinois, Indiana, Iowa, Michigan, Michigan State, Minnesota, Northwestern, Purdue, Ohio State, and Wisconsin.

Ivy League—Brown, Columbia, Cornell, Dartmouth, Harvard, Pennsylvania, Princeton, and Yale.

Mid-American—Ball State, Bowling Green, Central Michigan, Eastern Michigan, Kent State, Miami, Northern Illinois, Ohio, Toledo, and Western Michigan.

Missouri Valley—Drake, Indiana State, New Mexico State, Southern Illinois, Tulsa, West Texas State, and Wichita State.

Pacific Ten—Arizona, Arizona State, University of California at Berkeley, Oregon, Oregon State, University of Southern California, Stanford, University of California at Los Angeles, Washington, and Washington State.

Pacific Coast Athletic—Fresno, Fullerton, Long Beach, Pacific, and San Jose.

Southeastern—Alabama, Auburn, Florida, Georgia, Kentucky, Louisiana State, Mississippi, Mississippi State, Tennessee, and Vanderbilt.

Southwest—Arkansas, Baylor, Houston, Rice, Southern Methodist, Texas,

OHIO STATE'S WOODY Hayes is a college football coaching institution.

Texas A & M, Texas Christian, and Texas Tech.

Western Athletic—Brigham Young, Colorado State, New Mexico, Texas-El Paso, Utah, and Wyoming.

Some major-college teams prefer to compete as independents. Among the more notable are: Army, Air Force, Navy, Notre Dame, Florida State, Penn State, Tulane, Pittsburgh, Utah State, and Syracuse.

The NCAA's Division II has approximately 125 teams. The schools typically are smaller than those in Division I, but there are exceptions. The primary difference between the two divisions involves commitment in financial assistance to the sport, scholarships, and eligibility requirements. Division I schools offer more scholarships and generally spend more money on football. The income also is bigger because of larger stadiums and television appearances.

Division III of the NCAA is made up of the balance of schools and teams, the smallest schools both in terms of enrollment and financial assistance for their programs.

Champions are determined at each NCAA level, but the manner differs. Actual playoffs are held each year in Division II and III at the conclusion of the regular season. The participants are selected by area committees and the schedule is organized so that both regional and at-large representatives are picked to participate. The Division II competition culminates in the annual Pioneer Bowl game. Division III has its windup in the Stagg Bowl contest.

A champion is not determined in such a clear-cut fashion for Division I because the NCAA does not officially recognize a champion. There are no Division I playoffs, but that day may not be far off.

Instead, a No. 1 team is unofficially decided through comparison of scores, past performances, and relative strengths and weaknesses by coaches and sportswriters in polls that are conducted by the Associated Press and the United Press news services during and after the season.

At the end of the regular season, the best teams are invited to participate in bowl games, and when those results are learned the final polls are conducted to arrive at a No. 1 team. Since there are no playoffs, however, this method of choosing a top team always is open to conjecture when there is no clear-cut winner.

The windup to the 1977 season was a classic example. The No. 1 rated team most of the year was Texas. It was followed, in order, in one poll (sportswriters) by Alabama, Oklahoma, Michigan, Notre Dame, Arkansas, Kentucky, Ohio State, Penn State, and Pittsburgh. In the other poll (coaches), the teams named after Texas were Oklahoma, Alabama, Michigan, Notre Dame. Arkansas. Ohio State, Penn State, Pittsburgh, and Nebraska.

Then, in the bowl games, Notre Dame swamped Texas. Alabama topped Ohio State, Arkansas whipped Oklahoma, Penn State defeated Arizona State, and Washington beat Michigan.

So what did the final poll show? It was Notre Dame, Alabama, Arkansas, Texas, Penn State, Kentucky, Oklahoma, Pittsburgh, Michigan, and Washington in the sportswriters' poll. The coaches' poll was Notre Dame, Alabama, Arkansas, Penn State, Texas, Oklahoma, Pittsburgh, Michigan, Washington, and Nebraska. The Alabama legislature declared its team No. 1 in a special proclamation.

The major bowl games at the end of the season are traditionally held on New Year's Day or New Year's Eve. They are the Cotton Bowl in Dallas (originated in 1937), the Orange Bowl in Miami (originated in 1933), the Rose Bowl in Pasadena, Calif. (originated 1902, played annu-

IT'S A SURE SIGN of victory when the members of the marching band put their hats on backwards for a post-game concert.

ally since 1916), and the Sugar Bowl in New Orleans (originated 1935). In addition, there are less prestigious bowl games that often play a role in the final ratings. These include: the Gator Bowl, the Fiesta Bowl, the Sun Bowl, the Astro-Bluebonnet Bowl, the Tangerine Bowl, the Peach Bowl, and the Liberty Bowl.

Some participants in bowl games are selected by prior arrangement with conferences and their champions, such as the Rose Bowl's contract with the Big Ten and Pacific Ten and the Cotton Bowl's arrangement with the Southwest Conference.

The NAIA has approximately 240 member schools with football teams, evenly split between the organization's own Division I and II. Playoffs are held each year to determine an official cham-

pion in each category. Although NAIA schools are not so well known as those in the NCAA because of their size and locations, each year this organization produces a number of excellent athletes who go on to pro football stardom. Examples are Ken Anderson (Cincinnati Bengals) of Augustana College (Ill.), Gene Upshaw (Oakland Raiders) of Texas A & I, Claude Humphrey (Atlanta Falcons) of Tennessee State, and Harvey Martin (Dallas Cowboys) of East Texas State.

The NJCAA has approximately 100 schools with football teams. There is no playoff at the end of the season, but there are several bowl games involving some schools.

Attendance at all college games has steadily grown since the early days, and today it is pushing the 34-million mark.

NOTRE DAME defeated Army 7–6 in this 1930 classic played before a capacity crowd in Chicago's Soldier Field.

EACH HALF of a football game begins with the kickoff, and here the offensive unit is lined up for just such a play.

RULES

The final score read Cornell 7, Dartmouth 3. The Big Red had rallied to avoid a major upset. Or had they? The winning touchdown in that 1940 game was scored on a last-second pass on a fifth down that mistakenly had been awarded the visitors by officials. The error of granting the illegal extra down was confirmed two days later in game films. The Eastern Intercollegiate Association ruled that no outside body had the power to change the score. It was up to the participants. All eyes turned to Cornell and Coach Red Blaik. After a brief huddle with school administrators, he sent a telegram: "Cornell relinquishes claim to its victory and extends congratulations to Dartmouth."

It is important to know the rules of any game you are playing, either to avoid penalties or more serious situations such as the 1940 Cornell-Dartmouth contest.

Explaining the rules of football can be difficult because the sport is governed by extensive regulations that may undergo change each season. A further complication is the variance of rules for professional, college, and other levels of football.

The basic rules will be outlined to give a better general understanding of the game and how it is played. Differences between the various levels will be pointed out only when it is important.

THE FIELD

A football field is a rectangular area 120 yards (360 feet) long and 53⅓ yards (160 feet) wide. Twenty yards (60 feet) of the length is distributed equally for end zones at each end of the field. The goal lines border end zones on the inside. The far borders of the end zones are end lines of the field.

The football field is further divided with lines parallel to the goal lines at five yard intervals (a first down in football was originally five yards), useful in marking first downs and penalties. Two lines parallel to the sidelines (70 feet, 9 inches from them in pro ball, 53 feet, 4 inches from them in college) are the inbounds lines. When a play goes out of bounds or the ball is dead between these inbounds lines and the sidelines, the ball is spotted for the next play on the nearest inbounds line.

Along each inbounds line each yard is marked from goal line. These "hash-marks" facilitate spotting the ball by officials.

Goalposts, in H-shaped configurations, are placed on the end lines midway from the sidelines at each end of the field. In pro football, the uprights of the goalposts are 18 feet, 6 inches apart, and the top face of the crossbar connecting the two posts must be 10 feet above the ground. In college ball, the goalposts are 23 feet, 4 inches wide, and the crossbar also is 10 feet off the ground. In the pros, the verticals above the crossbar extend at least 30 feet above it. In college, they extend at least 10 feet above the crossbar.

THE BALL

Traditionally a football has been referred to as a pigskin. In fact, it is made of cowhide or a composition called "rubber."

The football is a spheroid with a cover of four panels of pebble-grained leather without corrugations other than seams. It has one set of eight equally spaced lacings (professional and college; 8 to 12, high school) and it is a natural tan color. College teams may use the "rubber" ball if both squads are in agreement.

When inflated, a football weighs between 14 and 15 ounces. It may be 11 to 11¼ inches from tip to tip, and 28 to 28½ inches in circumference.

SCORING

The object of the game is to score more points than the opposition. If the score is tied at the conclusion of regulation time, an overtime may be played on some occasions to determine a victor.

A FOOTBALL FIELD is 100 yards long from goal line to goal line; the end zones are an additional 10 yards each.

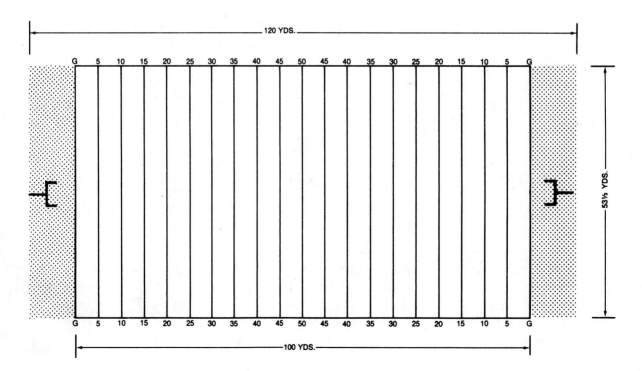

This is the practice in pro football during exhibition and regular season games when there is an extra 15-minute period of sudden-death play. The first team to score in this added period is the winner. If there is no score in the extra period, the game is a tie. In playoff games, however, there are as many extra periods as are needed until one of the teams can score.

There are four ways to score points.

A touchdown, six points, is scored when a legal forward pass is completed or a fumble or backward pass is caught by a defensive player on or behind the opponent's goal line; or when an offensive player is otherwise legally in possession of the ball while any part of it is on, above, or behind the opponent's goal line.

When a touchdown is scored, the scoring team has an opportunity to score an extra point or points with the clock stopped. This play, conversion as it is called, starts from the opponent's 2-yard line in professional football and the 3-yard line in college.

A placekick conversion counts for a single point when the ball is kicked between the uprights of the goalposts and above the crossbar. In college football, however, if the ball is run or passed over the goal line the play counts for two points.

A team with the ball also can score three points for kicking a field goal with either a placekick or a dropkick. (The dropkick has been rare since the ball was elongated in the 1930s to make passing easier.) Again, the ball must pass over the crossbar between the uprights of the opponent's goalpost before touching the ground.

Following a conversion try or a successful field goal, the ball is put in play again with a kickoff by the scoring team. If a field goal attempt is missed, however, the ball is turned over to the opposition at the scrimmage line where the attempt originated in pro games if the kick was from outside the 20-yard line. In college ball, the opponent takes over on its own 20-yard line after a missed field goal.

Two points are scored for a safety, which occurs when the ball becomes dead in the possession of an offensive player on, above, or behind his own goal line and the defending team is responsible for the ball being on that spot. After a safety, the team that had the two points scored against it then must put the ball back in play from its own 20-yard line with a punt, dropkick, or placekick toward its opponents' goal. The opponents must line up behind their own 30-yard line.

THE GAME

All professional and college games are 60 minutes long in playing time, divided into 15-minute quarters—or periods. There is a 15- to 20-minute intermission at the halfway point in college ball, but it can be shortened or lengthened by agreement of both teams. The pros have a 20-minute halftime.

Each half of the game starts with a kickoff.

Which team kicks or receives, and in what direction, is determined by the toss of a coin before the opening kickoff. Before the start of the second half, the order of choosing options is reversed.

Between the first and second quarters and also the third and fourth periods, there is a one-minute break; the teams switch directions and defend opposite goal lines.

The clock is stopped for penalties, scores, incomplete passes, injuries, television commercials, first downs, when the ball is out of bounds, and time outs. It starts again, except for extra-point tries, with the snap of the ball, or when an official indicates.

Each team gets three time outs for each half of play.

Ball in Play

A play starts with a snap from center in scrimmage play or a kick and the ball is considered dead when an official declares it so by sounding his whistle. A snap is handing or passing the ball from its position on the ground with a quick and continuous motion of the hand or hands of the center.

The official declares the ball dead when the runner is held so that his forward progress stops, when the runner scores or goes out of bounds, a kick receiver makes a fair catch, or the ball hits the ground following an incomplete pass.

A player is out of bounds when any part of his body touches anything other than another player or game official who is on or outside a boundary line. A player cannot return to the field to catch a pass once he has been out of bounds.

A ball in player possession is considered out of bounds when either the ball or any part of the runner touches the ground or anything else, which is on or outside a boundary line except another player or game official. Also, a receiver must have both feet inbounds (professional; one foot, college) and possession of the ball for a pass to be ruled complete.

A series of four consecutive scrimmage downs is awarded the team which is next to put the ball in play with a snap after a kickoff or a change in possession. A down is a unit of the game which starts after the ball is ready for play with a snap and ends when the ball is dead.

The scrimmage line is an imaginary line connecting the ball at a right angle with the sidelines.

After taking possession of the ball, the offensive team has four downs to advance it a minimum of ten yards. If it is successful, the team retains the ball for another set of four downs. If it is not successful, the defensive team takes possession following the fourth down. In most cases, the offensive team punts the ball if it is facing fourth down and long yardage in order to gain better field position than the point at which it would have to give it up.

Possession also changes with a kick following a score. A kickoff after a touchdown or field goal takes place at the 35-yard line of the kicking team in the pro games and the 40-yard line in college games.

After the football is ready for play and before the snap, each player or entering substitute of a team must have been within 15 yards of the ball and no simulated replacement of a player is to be used to confuse opponents.

When the football is snapped, the offense must be in a formation that meets these requirements: at least seven players must be on the scrimmage line; all players must be in bounds and behind the scrimmage line; and one player may be in motion, but not in motion toward his opponent's goal line, while all of his teammates must remain stationary with no movement of any part of their body.

If a snap is preceded by a huddle or shift, all players of the offensive team must come to an absolute stop and remain stationary for at least one full second.

The ball must not be handed forward to a teammate unless the exchange takes place behind the line of scrimmage. A runner may hand or pass the ball backward at any time, except to throw it intentionally out of bounds to conserve time. But, the backward pass—or fumble—may be caught or recovered by any player who is inbounds.

A team may make one forward pass during each down provided the pass is thrown from a point behind the scrimmage line. Any offensive player who lines up on the end of his scrimmage line or a back is eligible to catch a pass. Any defensive player is eligible to intercept a pass. A receiver for the offense cannot be interfered with while the football is in the air (defensive interference). Likewise, the receiver cannot interfere with a defender's progress at catching the ball once it is in the air (offensive interference).

PENALTIES

Many infractions of the rules may occur during a game and penalties commonly may range from a loss of 5 to 15 yards to the loss of a down.

Here is a list of some of the more frequently called infractions which occur during games: Offsides (when a player crosses the scrimmage line before the snap); delay of game; more than 11 players on the field; illegal motion (moving in the wrong direction—or moving at all, in some cases—before the snap); illegal procedure (employing an illegal alignment); illegal use of hands (blockers are not permitted to use their hands); pass interference; holding; clipping (blocking someone from behind); roughing the kicker; roughing the passer; grabbing a facemask; tripping; hurdling (jumping over a player); unnecessary roughness; and unsportsmanlike conduct.

AN ILLINOIS STATE quarterback has his sights set squarely on a teammate downfield on this pass play.

chapter 3
OFFENSIVE POSITIONS

The Minnesota Vikings had the first draft pick in 1968, and they bypassed many potentially flashy stars such as Larry Csonka, Greg Landry, Rocky Bleier, Earl McCullouch, Charlie Sanders, MacArthur Lane, Virgil Carter, and Jesse Phillips to get what they wanted. Their choice was Ron Yary, a big tackle from Southern California. The Vikings had been a losing team the previous season, but with Yary anchoring the offensive line they won a division title in his rookie year. He has been a fixture ever since.

There can be only 11 players on the field for one team, and each athlete, whether on offense or defense, has a specific position.

The responsibilities of these positions have drastically changed over the years as the game itself changed. Today the duties even differ from team to team depending on the formations employed.

The positions of offensive players fall into three classes: backfield (quarterback, halfbacks, fullback), interior line (center, two guards, and two tackles), and receivers (tight end and wide receiver). Sometimes there is overlap.

BACKFIELD

The backfield receives most of the adulation because it scores most of the points and gains many of the yards.

Quarterback

The quarterback is the hub of the offense. He calls signals at the line of scrimmage, takes the snap from the center, and sets the plays in motion.

In effect, the quarterback is the middleman between the coaching staff and the team on the field. Sometimes a quarterback has the responsibility of calling his own plays on the field. Usually, however, plays are sent in to him by substitutes serving as messengers.

To take the snap from center, the quarterback lines up directly behind him while

THE QUARTERBACK SETS each play in motion by taking the snap from his center.

THE CENTER'S SNAP to the quarterback should be an effortless, crisp exchange.

A QUARTERBACK sets up to launch his pass.

he is bending over the football. The play starts when the center passes the ball to the quarterback through his legs on a predetermined signal established in the huddle before each play. Signals should be called with a crisp, clear voice, and the count should be varied each down to prevent the defense from knowing when the ball will be passed.

Sometimes the quarterback calls an audible, a signal to alter the play, at the line of scrimmage. Audibles are called because a quarterback has spotted a particular variance in the defensive alignment after he has taken his position behind the center. Teams have special codes for audibles.

After taking the snap from center, the quarterback puts the play into execution as deceptively and smoothly as possible in order to upset the defense. A direct handoff or lateral to another back must be timed so that not a step is wasted. For a pass, the quarterback needs to drop back quickly from the line of scrimmage to the correct passing spot as quickly as possible to look for receivers while evading charging defensive players.

The quarterback takes charge in the huddles and sees that there are no delays. He must be a leader who demonstrates poise and confidence while coordinating the efforts—and morale—of 10 teammates on the field.

Running Backs

By position, there are three running backs who form the backfield with the quarterback. Running backs can have quite different duties, however.

THIS QUARTERBACK guarantees a good exchange by planting the football firmly into the grasp of a teammate on the handoff.

THE KIND OF EXTRA effort demonstrated by this Texas A & M running back sometimes can mean the difference between victory and defeat.

THIS IOWA STATE running back provides a big target for the quarterback on the handoff.

One of the running backs, usually called the fullback, is the power runner. The fullback's chief responsibilities include running with the ball anywhere from 15 to 30 times a game, faking runs, and blocking. Occasionally, he will catch a pass. Most of the fullback's running is off tackle or through the center of the line in short yardage situations.

The other two running backs in the backfield have traditionally been called halfbacks, but their duties can vary greatly from team to team. One halfback usually shares many of the fullback's responsibilities. This halfback, however, is likely to be a little speedier than the fullback so that with his teammates' help he can get away from the close quarters of the interior line. Thus the halfback complements the fullback and makes it tougher for the defense to key on one player and one area. If he is quicker than the fullback, his speed can be more effective if he gets quickly to an area of fewer defenders where there is more running room. The halfback is also likely to be called on to catch passes in addition to blocking.

The running back typically assumes a three-point stance at the start of each play. This means he bends over with his feet approximately shoulder-width apart and one hand touching the ground, supporting about a fourth of his weight as the third point in the stance. Sometimes a running back will not touch the ground with his hand, but will bend over slightly to facilitate a quick start. Sometimes a running back will use a four-point stance with both hands on the ground. Whatever the stance, it is important for the running back to be consistent so as not to tip off the opposition by varying his stance in the direction he will be heading.

Sometimes a running back is talented enough to effectively combine the skills that it takes to be both halfback and fullback. A classic example has been the Chicago Bears' Walter Payton, who has led the National Football Conference in rushing the last two seasons. Payton is fast enough to be an effective halfback running to the outside, and he is also strong enough to be used in the middle.

The final member of the backfield sometimes is not a running back at all. Often called the flankerback, he lines up at least five yards to either side of his backfield teammates. This back's main responsibilities are to go downfield to catch passes or to block for the running back. The flanker spends little time at the line of scrimmage, but will sometimes be called on to run with the ball, usually on a deceptive play designed to take advantage of his speed.

INTERIOR LINEMEN

Center

The center handles the ball as much as anyone on the field because it is his snap to the quarterback for scrimmage play, and to the punter or holder for a place-kick that starts every play. The snaps, to be coordinated with the quarterback's predetermined signal for them, are the center's chief duties.

After the snap, blocking becomes the center's added job. Usually the blocking is against the defensive middle linemen, but sometimes, because defensive linemen have an advantage in getting past while the ball is being centered, the center's blocking is directed at defenders beyond the line of scrimmage.

Guards

The two offensive guards, right and left, line up next to the center. Guards usually use the three-point stance but occasionally will go into a four-pointer when digging in to get under opponents.

A guard's energies are devoted exclusively to blocking, mostly at the line of scrimmage, unless the guard is called on to pull from his spot on the line and lead blocking downfield or on a running play around end. In addition, the guards drop back to protect the quarterback on pass plays.

Tackles

The two tackles line up on the outside of the guards. A tackle has almost the same assignments as the guards and uses the same stances.

RECEIVERS

Tight End

Every team usually has at least one end who lines up close to a tackle, called a tight end. Sometimes, especially on inside running plays which require plenty of interior blocking, a team will station two such ends on the line. In this case, technically, they would be the right and left ends.

Most teams, especially among the pros, have only one tight end, who is called on to help with much of the blocking both at the line of scrimmage and beyond. He will also be a pass receiver—usually of short passes. Tight end is considered one of the toughest in the sport since he does everything but pass the ball.

Split End

The split end is also on the line of scrimmage because there must be at least seven offensive players there for every play. As a split end, however, he lines up at least several yards away from the nearest tackle. His primary job is as a pass receiver and blocker downfield. Usually, a split end is one of the fastest players on the offense and is called on to simply outrun defenders. If he cannot, he must use deception to get free to catch passes. The split end also is referred to as a wide receiver.

HERE IS THE entire offense in a wishbone formation. The linemen have assumed their three-point stances while the backs also are prepared for the start of the play.

THE MISSOURI QUARTERBACK and running back have time for a handoff because the offensive line keeps the defense from penetrating.

PURDUE RECEIVER Paul Beery shows that catching a pass is not always easy, especially when the quarterback is off target.

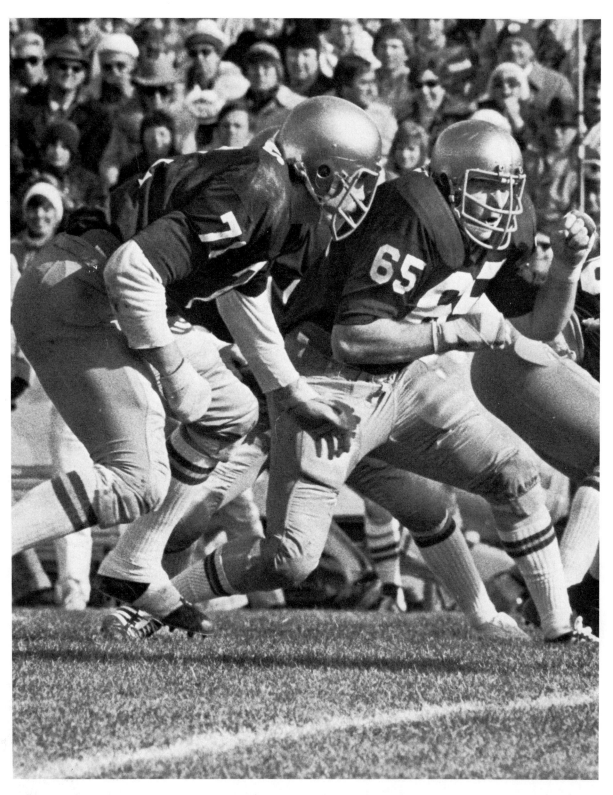

NOTRE DAME OFFENSIVE linemen Steve McDaniels (71) and Ernie Hughes (65) set up a blocking wall by backing off from the line of scrimmage.

chapter 4
BLOCKING

There were 16 seconds remaining in the 1967 NFL title game when Green Bay's Bart Starr plunged over from the 1-yard line on fourth down to give the Packers a 21-17 victory over Dallas. It was to be the final championship for Green Bay Coach Vince Lombardi, and it came on a day when the thermometer read 13 degrees below zero and the wind gusts were close to 20 miles per hour. But it also was a day in which the most celebrated player was Green Bay's offensive guard Jerry Kramer, whose crucial block of Jethro Pugh opened the way into the end zone for Starr. The dramatic play by Kramer was captured on film, and before the afternoon was over Kramer's block earned him headlines in sport pages around the country. It was the rarest of moments for an offensive lineman.

Blocking occurs when an offensive player without the football serves as an obstruction to a defensive player trying to stop the ball carrier.

Obviously blocking is the foundation for a good offense because without it there would be little chance to advance the football. Good blocking enhances the offense's chances for longer gains.

Because the blocker's goal is to serve as interference, the more tacklers that can be obstructed leaves the fewer there are to stop the ball carrier.

A blocker has inherent advantages. For one thing, he knows in which direction the play is going and that information makes it easier for him to determine his approach to neutralize a defensive player. Also, knowing the play means the blocker will know how long an opponent must be detained.

On the other hand, rules limit what a blocker can do. The blocker cannot use his hands and he cannot make contact from behind the defensive player in certain areas of the field. Blocking therefore must be a very precise and difficult maneuver at times.

The one important question as to how

OFFENSIVE LINEMEN quickly move to their blocking assignments following the snap of the football.

ARKANSAS QUARTERBACK Ron Calcagni effectively uses a teammate as a blocker.

AN ILLINOIS RUNNING back (22) prepares to take a pitch and follow his blockers.

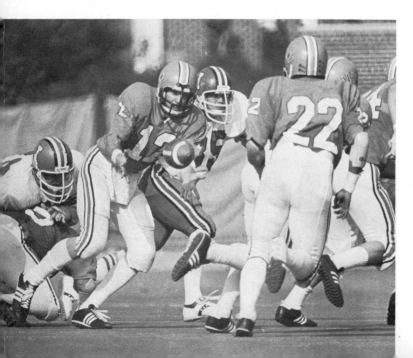

a blocker approaches defensive players is determined by where the block is to take place on the field. Different techniques are needed for blocks in close quarters near the scrimmage line than for blocks in downfield areas. Additionally, a blocker's objectives will depend greatly on the type of play being run.

Blocking is perhaps the least glamorous aspect of football because few spectators notice it. Everyone likes to follow the football, not the players in front and around it. As a result, it takes a particularly dedicated player to be a good blocker. Coaches, however, recognize the value of blocking. It is no coincidence that some of the best teams of recent decades had excellent offensive lines to open the way for the more highly publicized runners or to protect the quarterback from the onrushing defensive line.

BLOCKING TECHNIQUES

Shoulder Block

The basic block in football is the shoulder block in which the shoulder is driven into an opponent's stomach or legs with the intention of knocking him down or moving him in a certain direction.

The shoulder block can be thrown from an entirely upright position or driven into an opponent as the blocker rises from his stance. Either way, it is advisable that the approach just before contact includes short, choppy steps to keep from losing one's balance or becoming overcommitted. If this block is used coming from the stance, one quick, short, backward step will help generate more momentum for another strong thrust forward. Sometimes, the shoulder is used for the block after contact is first made with the defensive lineman's helmet.

In blocking, the follow-through is important, especially when the defender still is standing and remains in position to make a tackle. If the shoulder block has

been made at the scrimmage line, the blocker may pull back after the initial charge and continue striking with short hits unless his assignment calls for vacating the area.

In a downfield, faster-moving situation, the blocker most likely will not have the luxury of being able to throw more than one shoulder block; therefore it is important not to miss.

Some tips: Concentrate on the initial charge. If it is strong enough at first, it is less likely the defensive player can recover to make a tackle. Also, the blocker should keep his head up and eyes open at all times in order to follow his opponent's moves and make any necessary counter moves.

Cross-Body Block

This block, also referred to as the cut-off block, must be used at very close range because there is no chance for recovery after the blocker has committed himself. In effect, the whole body in a horizontal position is used to knock the defender's legs out from under him.

The cross-body block starts as if it were a shoulder block. But instead of the shoulder making contact, it slides by the defender and the blocker leaves his feet, using the side of his body to bring down or detain his man. The danger is that once the blocker is off the ground, it takes more time for him to recover and get back into the play. Therefore it is important to make the block work.

A cross-body block used at the snap on the line of scrimmage does not require the blocker to rise up and start the sequence. He can be just as effective by simply lunging from his stance toward his opponent's legs.

Some tips: The whole length of the body can be used so that if the upper body misses, it is entirely possible to cut down the defensive player with hips, thighs, or legs—anything short of deliberately tripping him.

Screen Block

It is not always essential to make contact with an opponent to obstruct him, especially in open spaces away from the scrimmage line. The screen block is merely an attempt to get between the ball carrier and the defender, making it hard for the tackler to see the runner—let alone stop him.

The screen block is usually effective beyond the line of scrimmage with everyone moving at full speed. Therefore the blocker should be alert to fakes by the defender because he cannot afford to waste time making contact with the blocker.

A screen block also can be a position block, in which, for instance, the blocker goes to a specific spot and positions himself to effectively cut off pursuit when the play comes his way.

Crab Block

The blocker will be down on all fours in the crab block trying to knock the defender off his feet by throwing himself at his ankles or knees. Such a block is used at the line of scrimmage—usually from a four-point stance—by simply crawling out to meet the defender. This block is particularly effective against a defender with the strength or size to thwart other blocks. Ideally, the defender can be delayed even longer by entangling legs with his.

Double team

When a defensive lineman is very difficult to block or other circumstances dictate, he may be double-teamed; that is, two men may be used.

Any one of these blocking styles may be used, but whichever is selected, blocks should complement each other. In other words, if one blocker hits the defender low the other should hit him high.

GAME SITUATIONS

It is one thing to describe how to block a defender and another to do it. Because blocking is such an important—and sometimes tough—task, it is often coordinated with teammates to achieve maximum results.

For instance, for an end run an offensive coach may have one or two of his linemen pulling from their positions to lead the interference. Other offensive linemen will make their block at the line and then go farther downfield to block one of the defensive backs.

Perhaps the play calls for the quarterback to drop back and throw a pass. In this case, the blockers will drop back from the line of scrimmage after making an initial contact with the defensive line to form a wall with other offensive blockers around the passer.

The following are some typical game situations that call for special coordination among blockers.

Blocking Kicks

If the kick is to be a punt, the offensive objective is to block the rushers at the line of scrimmage. The offense cannot afford to linger too long, however, as very quickly the offensive player will become a defensive player trying to stop the punt receiver. It is advisable, therefore, in many cases to brush block, which means to make only enough contact with the onrushing defensive lineman to momentarily delay him before heading downfield to cover the punt.

The quicker the punter can get off the kick, the less time his blockers will have to spend blocking. Usually an additional blocker will be stationed near the kicker

SOMETIMES IT IS an effective measure to double-team a defender on a block.

THESE HIGH SCHOOL blockers do an effective job of forming a wall to prevent the defense from stopping a placekick.

as a safeguard against any rushers who have gotten through the line defenses quick enough to block the kick.

If the kick is to be a placekick for an extra point or field goal, the blocker will be required to spend more time at the line of scrimmage. This need occurs because the kicker will be closer to the line to shorten the distance as much as possible. In this case, the blocker's best approach is to plant himself squarely to meet the rusher head-on.

Pass Blocking

Protecting the passer is important for two big reasons: The payoff usually is big if the pass can be completed, and there is greater risk because if the quarterback is tackled before he can throw the football, there is a sizable loss of yardage, or worse yet, a fumble.

In pass blocking it is important for the blocker to stay on his feet as long as possible so that he can protect the passer long enough for him to spot a receiver and throw. Thus it is best for the blocker to make contact, retreat, and set for another hit—and repeat the process again. As a result of this sequence, by the time the nucleus of linemen has repeated it several times, they are consolidated into a wall around the quarterback in his pocket of protection. Sometimes the quarterback is a scrambler, preferring to move around behind the line of scrimmage looking for targets instead of staying in the pocket. A scrambler complicates the blocker's job, and in most cases the most effective method is a simple man-to-man approach in which offensive players have a predetermined defensive player to guard.

Trap Blocking

Many times an offensive lineman simply will leave his spot and let a defender through so that he can be blocked more effectively by someone else, perhaps a running back or another lineman. This trap is a good maneuver against a defender who is especially tough to contain. Or, it is one way of creating a hole in the line for a draw play.

Downfield Blocking

Throwing a block downfield can be difficult because the defender often has more room in which to maneuver and avoid the blocker. The payoff, however, can be great because very often it takes only one downfield block to spring the runner loose for a touchdown.

Whatever it takes to obstruct the defender—short of an illegal move—is applicable downfield because by this time the ball carrier most likely has generated enough speed so that he will need only the slightest assistance to get past the tackler.

HOW TO PRACTICE

Working on individual blocking techniques is not a very complicated task. All it takes is two players. Ideally, it is good to work against a variety of persons who offer a variety of problems. This method is helpful because it is what you will be facing in a game. Practice with blocking dummies is also helpful. Most teams have large stationary ones to work on individually and also some mounted on sleds for team efforts.

Many mechanical devices are available, but costs can be kept down by just using some imagination. For example, a simple bar can be held off the ground by two players for blockers to pass underneath in order to practice staying low on their approaches. Heavy pads can be wrapped around trees or other large objects for blockers to hit and toughen themselves for live contact.

Unfortunately, working on blocking is a tedious chore full of repetition. Because of the importance of blocking, however, it is something that has to be constantly practiced.

ILLEGAL BLOCKING

Blocking is something that is watched very closely by officials. It is a good idea, therefore, to become familiar with what constitutes a legitimate block and what does not.

Clipping

Clipping is probably one of the most obvious rule infractions. It occurs when a blocker hits a defender from behind. A 15-yard penalty is assessed for the foul. There are zones adjacent to the scrimmage line (they differ in pro and college football) near the center of action, however, where it is legal to clip.

Use of Hands

A blocker cannot use his hands. Doing so will result in a 15-yard penalty, too.

Holding

A blocker cannot hold a defender with any part of his body. For instance, it is not legal to lie on top of an opponent to prevent him from making progress toward a tackle. Nor can he hold on to any part of his uniform or equipment. Doing so incurs a 15-yard penalty.

Tripping

It is illegal to trip anyone on the field and the penalty is 15 yards.

Locking

It is illegal for blockers to link their bodies together in any manner to create a larger obstruction. The penalty is 15 yards.

HEAVY ARM PADS are a good way to prevent injuries during practice.

RUNNING BACKS HELP with blocking, too, and here one moves to protect his quarterback from a charging defensive lineman.

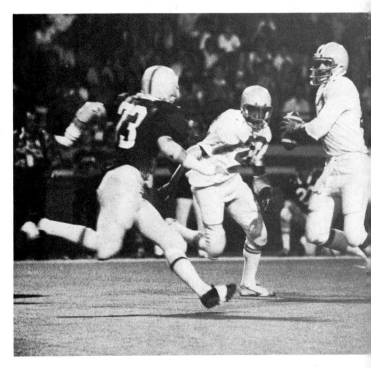

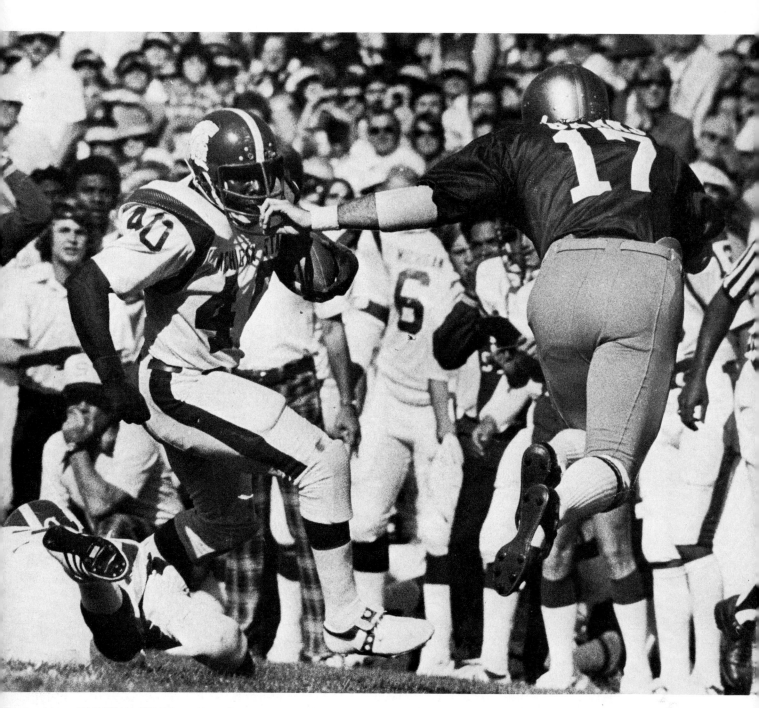

MICHIGAN STATE vs. Notre Dame is one of the country's great college rivalries. State running back Levi Jackson breaks loose for a gain in this recent rematch.

chapter 5
RUNNING

The shifty running back had firmly established himself as All-American material in his first season of college football. He ran for three touchdowns in 39 minutes in his opening game and then went on to help his team win two more games that year with long runs. But no one was quite prepared the second season for his effort against a Michigan squad which hadn't lost in three years. He danced and weaved his way to a 44-yard touchdown run for openers and within the next 12 minutes added scoring gallops of 56, 67, and 95 yards. It was the greatest individual effort ever by a college player. Red Grange, in leading Illinois to a 39–14 win, had left no doubt about his credentials.—October 18, 1924

It is no coincidence that most football teams run with the football more than they try to pass. This is because a good running attack means that a team will exercise more control of the ball, and the more a team has the ball the less opportunity the opponent will have to score.

This is the goal of every coach.

Additionally, a running attack usually is simpler to teach than a passing game because more players are adept at running than at passing.

Conversely, coaches usually don't want their teams to pass the football as often as they run with it because there is less control of possession, interceptions are always a threat, and it is more difficult to find players capable of implementing a good passing attack.

For these and other reasons, the running game usually is considered the foundation for the entire offense. If a team can successfully run with the football, it makes it easier to have a passing threat because the defense has to concentrate on stopping the ground game. Also, a strong running game makes play-action fakes (plays that seem to start as a run or pass and turn into the other), draw plays, and screen passes even more effective.

The ideal situation that coaches seek is an offense with a good blend of passing and running. Most championship teams

PENN STATE RUNNING back Matt Su-
hey prepares to make a cut.

THIS ILLINOIS RUNNER demonstrates that a good back doesn't always need a lot
of room to sneak through the defense.

have this mixture unless they are so strong at just one phase that the opposition cannot stop it. The Big Ten Conference, a run-conscious league, is a good example. Ohio State and Michigan have dominated the conference with their exceptionally strong running attacks so much in recent years that they have not needed to pass to win. Of course, Big Ten champions have not done so well in the Rose Bowl recently.

There are basically three types of running attacks: power, finesse, and a combination of the two.

POWER RUNNING

The power attack revolves around runs that are directed into the line where strength is more important than deception. The purpose usually is to gain yardage by running over and through opponents at the scrimmage line. Power running most often is used in short yardage situations (when two or three yards are needed for first down) or near the goal line.

The successful power-running team eventually should physically tire the opposition's defense. Speed is not an essential ingredient in the power-running game because blockers and runner will be operating in close quarters. Once the ball

carrier can get past the scrimmage line, however, his chances for a sizable gain will be enhanced if he is swift.

In the power attack, success will be greatly determined by the blockers and the ability of the running back to break tackles. Every blocker usually has a specific assignment on running plays, and in a power play there should be little time wasted getting to an opponent in order to take advantage of momentum with the snap.

Some typical power running plays are: off tackle, quarterback sneak, and sweep.

The off-tackle play means exactly what it says. The running back, after taking a handoff from the quarterback, runs into the line at the tackle slot where, hopefully, the offensive tackle has moved the defensive lineman out of the path of the runner.

The quarterback sneak typically is employed when only a yard or two is needed. The quarterback simply takes the snap and follows his center straight up the middle.

The sweep is a wider running play in which the runner usually moves parallel to the line of scrimmage until he can turn the corner and cut downfield. The key to success is getting enough blockers in front of the runner before the defense adjusts.

TEXAS HAS BEEN blessed with many fine running backs; Johnny Ham Jones ranks among the fastest, as this tackler is about to learn.

TEXAS QUARTERBACK Sam Ansley cuts through a big hole on this keeper play.

A FLEET RUNNING back such as Roland Sales of Arkansas becomes a real threat once he is able to start putting defenders behind him.

FINESSE RUNNING

In the finesse attack, the emphasis is on deception and outflanking the opponent. Every squad should work on this attack because it is particularly useful against bigger, stronger teams that are more capable of outmuscling blockers.

The prime ingredient for this approach is ball carriers who rely more on angle and speed. The blockers also have to be quick. It is useless to devise fancy blocking assignments and time-consuming deception if the runners are not fast enough to take advantage of it all.

Some typical components of a finesse running play include pulling blockers, fakes, and misdirection. For instance, if plays are directed at the flanks, it is a waste of time and effort for some blockers to remain in the line when the flow of the play will be away from them. In other words, when a play is going around the right end, blockers from the left side of the line can pull from their positions and concentrate their efforts on linebackers or defensive ends and backs to give the ball carrier more room to maneuver.

Deception is a vital part of finesse running. The more tacklers that can be committed to stopping a play they see developing, the more effective it is for the offensive team to turn the play into a fake by taking advantage of the defensive commitment.

Sometimes a little misdirection is the best way to give a ball carrier more running room. By this, a play that appears to be going in one direction is reversed to go in another. The tackler's momentum carries the defenders away from the play. Misdirection can be applied, for example, by starting an end run to the right side only to have the ball carrier hand the football off at the last second to a running back, flanker, or tight end going in an opposite direction.

Some typical finesse plays are the trap, draw, pitch, and reverse.

The trap occurs when a defensive player is allowed to come through the offensive line and then is blocked when he tries to recover. A defensive tackle charges unmolested through the line and then he is blocked by a running back or pulling lineman. Because the defensive tackle is allowed to get into the offensive backfield, a hole in the defensive line is created.

The most common draw play is one in which the quarterback drops back as if to pass. Instead of throwing the ball, however, he hands off to a back who delays a second or two after the snap, and the would-be tacklers, thinking it is going to be a pass, are usually not in position to stop the run.

A pitch is a good way to spring a ball carrier away from a defensive line that consistently makes good penetration. Here, the quarterback simply laterals the football to one side to a running back, who thus already has the advantage of several steps toward getting away from onrushing defensive players.

The reverse play is time-consuming, but it also can be very effective when it is used at the right point during a game. Reverse plays are rarely used more than once or twice a game. In most cases, the quarterback starts the play by handing the football to a running back going laterally behind the line of scrimmage in the opposite direction the quarterback is heading. This change in direction for the ball can be compounded by the running back handing off again to another back going in the opposite direction the first ball carrier is heading. This is called a double reverse.

Variations can be run off the reverse such as faking some of the handoffs. The key to the play's execution, however, is smooth ball handling with as much deception as possible by the participants to confuse the defense.

TECHNIQUES

Many skills are needed for a football player to be a good runner: speed, power, balance, peripheral vision, timing, shiftiness.

Obviously, some skills can be taught and improved through hard work. Some skills, however, a good runner must almost be born with—and only more hard work can help a runner overcome whatever shortcoming he may possess.

Running ability can be greatly improved by a few simple techniques.

Carrying the Football

It is important to carry the football correctly because failure to do so often results in fumbles. The ball carrier should never hold the ball too far from his body because doing so makes it easier for tacklers to knock it loose from his grasp. Instead, the best way is to carry the ball length-wise, tucked away close to the body, shifting it to the side opposite approaching tacklers whenever possible. For instance, a ball carrier running along the right sideline should carry the ball on his right side. When running in close quarters—particularly on plunges into the line—it is always a good idea to wrap both arms around the ball and tuck it into the midsection.

Straight Arm

The straight arm is almost a forgotten weapon. It is a jabbing motion with your free hand and arm directed at the tackler, in effect, pushing him away. It's an especially effective technique in a one-on-one situation.

NOTRE DAME RUNNING back Vegas Ferguson has the football firmly in his grasp before making contact with this tackler.

THIS ARKANSAS RUNNING back cradles the football on the side opposite from where he is about to make contact with defensive players.

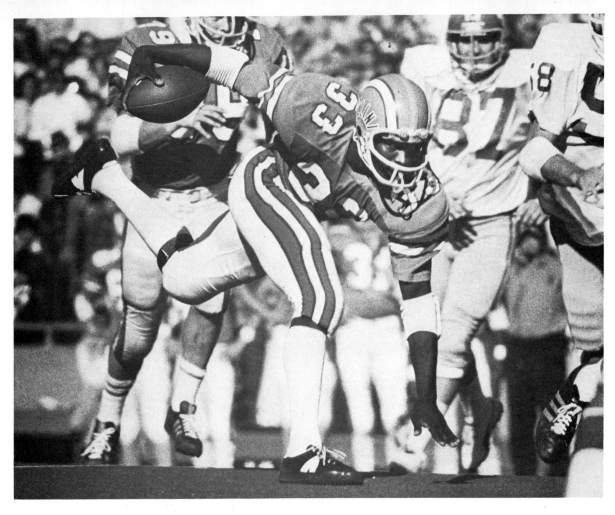

IT ISN'T ALWAYS easy to keep your balance, as this Illini runner discovers.

AN ILLINOIS RUNNING back zips past a fallen would-be tackler after making his cut upfield.

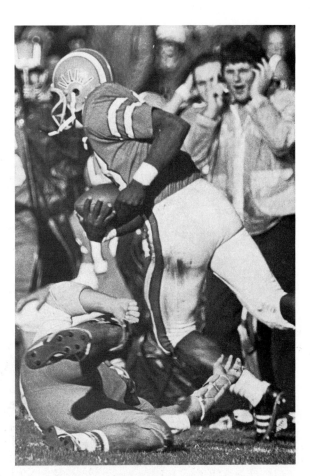

Change of Pace

The baseball pitcher has a change of pace and so can the runner. They are similar. In football, a runner may give the appearance of running at top speed while actually holding back. When a tackler is trying to time his move from a lateral approach, he simply shifts into high gear. Sometimes the opposite is effective: slowing down from full speed.

Using Blockers

The good runner should do everything he can to work as a team with his blockers because they can move potential tacklers out of the way. By veering or cutting, the runner may try to bring the defender's intercept line into the path of his blocking teammate. The runner must also work at taking off from the block in a direction away from the traffic congestion of defensive players.

Balance

A runner should try to keep his feet underneath him at all times. He must also work at bringing his knees up and keeping his feet apart. This combination makes it more difficult for the tackler.

Cutting

This maneuver means a change of direction while the runner keeps his entire body in control. On some outside plays, backs often make the mistake of trying to get outside the entire defense when they actually are better off cutting straight upfield. The cut can come at a sharp angle, or can be made as a gradual shift. But keep it simple.

Getting Hit

Usually it is possible for the runner to turn and twist after the initial contact by the tackler. He may try to squirm away to all the extra yardage he can get, but he should not do so at the expense of injuring an exposed knee or ankle. He should protect the ball at all times. Sometimes the runner is better off when he can see the hit by a defender developing to meet it head-on instead of taking it like a punching bag or tackling dummy. A runner should not go out of his way looking for hits, though.

IT'S DIFFICULT TO gain yards when you can't see where you're running, as this Northwestern back learns.

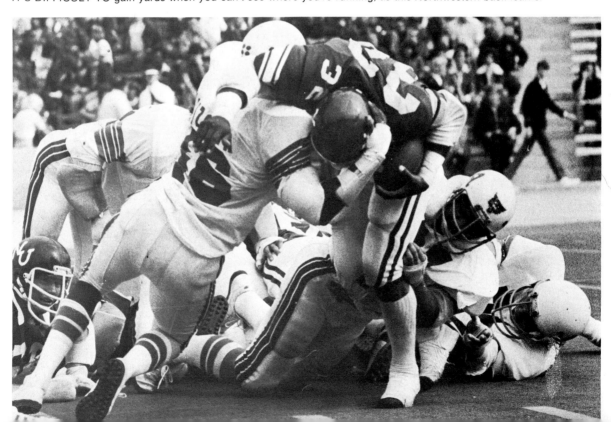

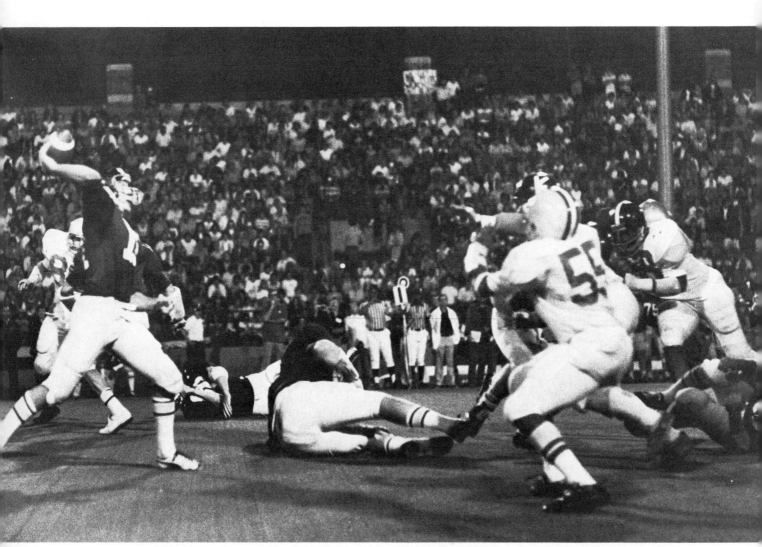

THIS HIGH SCHOOL quarterback displays excellent form in launching a pass behind plenty of protection.

chapter 6
PASSING

Notre Dame has had many outstanding quarterbacks. Tom Clements wasn't the greatest, but he did come through with one of the greatest passes ever thrown by a Fighting Irish player. In the 1973 Sugar Bowl, Alabama was trying to pin the first loss of the season on Clements' team and thereby deny it the national championship. Notre Dame was leading by a slim margin of 24–23 with just over 2 minutes remaining, but on third down and long yardage to go on its own 2 the situation was desperate. One more down and the Irish would have to punt from their end zone to the Crimson Tide. Clements dropped back deep into the end zone with the snap, dodged several rushers, and uncorked a perfect pass to right end Robin Weber racing down the sideline. It was good for a 30-yard gain, breathing room, and the national championship.

Woody Hayes, the Ohio State sage, is fond of saying that only three things can happen when you pass the football and two are bad. (It can be complete, incomplete, or intercepted.)

True as Woody's saying is, with hard work and some imagination completions can outnumber interceptions and incompletions. An effective passing game is the most dangerous weapon in football. It gives a team the capability of striking for long gains in a short period of time.

It is no coincidence that skilled passing occurs most often in professional football. To put the ball in the air with success requires the players' maximum effort in deception, speed, timing, discipline, accuracy, strength, concentration, and, in many cases, courage. In short, a pass play requires coordination of more skills by more players than just about any other move an offensive team can make.

Successful passing means plenty of practice; teams frequently spend more practice time on passing than any other part of the game. Once a passing attack has been put together, though, it is even more difficult for the defense to stop.

ARKANSAS QUARTERBACK Ron Calcagni lofts a swing pass to Roland Sales in a 31–6 victory over Oklahoma.

THIS IOWA STATE quarterback plants his left foot firmly on the ground before hurling his pass.

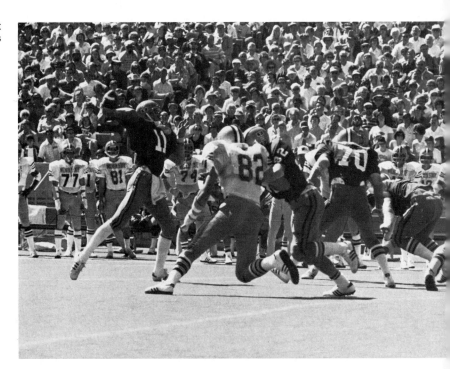

THIS ARIZONA QUARTERBACK manages to get his pass off despite harassment from the defense.

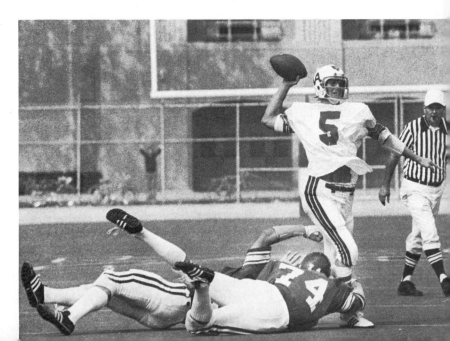

The passing attack of any team can be broken down into four major parts.

THE PASSER

Obviously, the passing game starts with the person throwing the football, who, in most cases, is the quarterback. Only occasionally will a running back or kicker throw, and then only to upset the defense.

A successful passer has to have certain physical attributes. For one thing, a successful passer needs to have height to see over onrushing defenders. In today's football it is almost inconceivable that anyone under six feet will become a successful passer. A successful passer needs a strong arm to throw both long and short passes with equal proficiency. Being able to throw both long and short makes it doubly tough for the defense because it has to concentrate on more than one area.

A good passer needn't have great speed, but he needs quick, sure feet to get set up in a hurry so that he has time to look for receivers. The successful passer should release the ball fast. Quick set-up and fast release cut the time required to complete the play.

A good passer needs good eyesight and especially good depth perception to locate targets at any spot on the field.

Finally, but perhaps most importantly, the passer should be tough and able to take his share of hard hits from rushers doing their damndest to stop the pass.

There are two stages in the actual throwing of the football: setting up and delivering.

Setting Up and Delivery

It is important to set up as quickly as possible so that there is more time to locate receivers. A quick set-up also puts less burden on blockers fending off would-be tacklers. The passer takes either backward or lateral steps in most cases,

and thus good balance is essential.

If the passer turns his back on the scrimmage line while setting up, he needs to keep glancing backward to check for any important developments that may affect the play's progress.

A passer should carry the ball tucked against his midsection with both hands to avoid fumbling while moving to the passing spot. The ball is gradually brought to passing height with the throwing arm by the time the passer reaches the passing spot.

The hand that is not used to throw the ball becomes a stabilizer and gives balance by its forward thrust as the throwing arm is cocked for a smooth overhand motion.

This motion should start with the ball grasped on the back one-third by the passing hand. The ends of the fingers should be on the laces to lend spin for a good spiral flight. The throwing movement should be led by the left leg being planted in the direction of the target if the passer is right-handed.

The entire stride, plus follow-through of the throwing arm, should be aimed toward the receiver. Assuming a sturdy, upright stance as a foundation for the pass gains maximum use of the legs as a source of power.

There are three basic routes the passer will take when throwing the ball: Drop back, roll out, or play-action. The latter two are worth a comment.

Roll Out

A passer who rolls out moves to the right or left to pass. Sometimes the ball is thrown on the run. Another variation is to sprint straight to one spot, and then set up for the play.

Play Action

A play-action pass develops from an in-

A QUARTERBACK gets rid of his pass moments before a tackler comes crashing through.

PENN STATE QUARTERBACK Chuck Fusina sprints toward the spot from where he'll eventually throw his pass.

CATCHING A PASS is not always easy, as this receiver learns from two defenders.

itial fake to a runner. Then the quarterback drops back to pass. The purpose of the first move is to commit the defense to a run, thus making it difficult for the defense to recover. One variation is the bootleg, where the ball is hidden on the hip or along the thigh opposite the rushers following a fake handoff to another back. The bootleg can be used effectively either to set up for a pass or as a running play.

PROTECTING THE PASSER

The best defense against a passing attack is to tackle the man with the ball before he passes it. Not only does this prevent a pass, it also will result in a sizable loss of yardage. When the defense tackles the quarterback behind the scrimmage line, it is called a sack.

Therefore, the offensive team can expect a determined rush on most passing plays, and protecting the man with the ball usually requires an all-out effort by the interior line and usually one or two backs.

Protecting the passer must be a coordinated effort in which each blocker assumes certain duties and then carefully performs them to avoid overlap with his fellow players.

In most instances the blockers form a wall around a pocket of protection for the passer while he looks for receivers. The blocker's job is to stay on his feet and gradually retreat into the wall, which typically is a semicircle, after making initial contacts with the rushers.

The running backs who remain behind as blockers usually are assigned the job of picking up any rushers who have avoided the linemen. In most cases, such rushers are a blitzing defensive back, an end who has outflanked the defense, or an exceptionally quick defensive lineman who simply has blown past a front blocker.

On the other hand, it is important that the passer effectively use his blockers by staying in the pocket. If he is a scrambler, such as Fran Tarkenton of the Minnesota Vikings, or a roll-out passer it will be necessary to plan alternative blocking assignments.

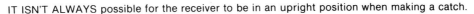

IT ISN'T ALWAYS possible for the receiver to be in an upright position when making a catch.

A RECEIVER NEEDS good hands to snare passes that aren't always on target.

RECEIVING

Some of football's most exciting moments occur on pass plays. Therefore, the players on the receiving end have a glamorous and headline winning job—if they catch the ball.

Two absolute prerequisites for a successful receiver are good hands and quick feet. Having "good hands" simply means the ability to catch and hang on to the ball.

Obviously he needs good hands. All pass catchers are expected to grab balls that come straight to them, but the exceptional performers are those who can snare off-target passes.

Getting in position to make the reception is the most important part of the job, and it isn't always necessary to have blinding speed—although it certainly never hurts to be quicker than your defender. Sometimes all it takes is just a quick fake to throw the defender offstride and then get ahead of him by one or two steps.

The ends and all backs are eligible to catch passes. In fact, if a player catches a ball thrown laterally or at a backward

NOTRE DAME GREAT Ken MacAfee stretches for a pass against Texas.

TEXAS SPLIT END Alfred Jackson looks upfield after making a catch.

angle behind the scrimmage line, it is legal for him to throw the ball, too, if he remains behind the line. However, it rarely happens.

Pass plays involve either long or short passes. Typically, running backs and tight ends are used for the passes closest to the scrimmage line. The flanker backs, split ends, and speedier running backs are used more as long-distance receivers.

All pass receivers have to run with the ball after they make the catch. A receiver cannot concentrate on running too much before he has the ball firmly in his grasp. The situation is similar to baseball's infielder thinking about his throw before he has the ball in the glove. Usually, failure to concentrate on catching the ball leads to an error in baseball, or a dropped pass in football, and the best way to avoid a dropped pass is to watch the ball sail into your hands.

Tight ends and backs making catches within close range have an advantage if they are blessed with strength to break tackles, for many of their catches will be in heavy traffic. On the other hand, speed and deception are important assets for a long-distance receiver to combat the moves of nimble defensive backs.

PATTERNS

For a passing team to be successful, the eligible receivers must run predetermined patterns, specified paths to the point the quarterback will throw to, thus helping the passer locate his targets. Patterns will vary according to the relative strengths and weaknesses of the receivers and of the defenders.

Discipline is vital in running patterns. When there are breakdowns, it means the passer needs more time to find receivers and this puts a strain on the entire offense. The passers and receivers must work hard together to coordinate their timing. In this way, the quarterback becomes more familiar with the moves of his receivers and consequently knows what to look for during a game. Likewise, the receivers should try to become so adept at running their patterns that they know exactly where and when to look for the ball when running them. The more passing and patterns can be coordinated, the better the chances of beating the defense.

Here are some of football's basic patterns, keeping in mind that many teams have their own names and variations.

Post

When within 20 or 30 yards of the goal line, the receiver goes straight down the field, usually for about 15 yards, and then makes a turn toward the goalpost. Many times the receiver fakes the post pattern before making his actual cut in the other direction.

Corner

The receiver runs downfield, again for about 15 yards, and then makes a turn toward the point where the goal line and sideline meet.

Fly

The fly pattern is merely a footrace for the end zone, and it is particularly effective if a receiver has good speed. He simply takes off from his offensive position, heads toward the side line and sprints toward the goal line with the intention of getting behind the deep backs.

Hook

The receiver bursts from his position—usually on the line—as if he were going straight downfield. Suddenly he makes a sharp turn back toward the scrimmage line to take what should be a hard, low pass.

Curl

This pattern starts out the same way as the hook, but here the receiver tries to get into the open area between the linebackers and deep backs when making the backward turn.

Look-In

This is where the quarterback hits the tight end with a short, quick pass right over the defensive line.

Sideline

The receiver, at just about any point after taking off from the scrimmage line, simply cuts to the sideline nearest him. Ideally, he is between the ball and the few defenders who will be guarding the outside zone. The danger is that if the ball is intercepted, there is usually no one in front of the defensive player to make a tackle.

Slant (In or Out)

The receiver, cutting off his outside foot, makes a quick turn into a slanting angle.

Flare

A pass to a receiver moving in to the outside area of the backfield, but not necessarily with a sharp angle.

Screen

The screen pass is thrown to the receiver usually behind the scrimmage line behind a blocking wall that has been formed before the ball arrives. Often the offensive line allows the defense to charge through to clear up congestion and help the blocking to set up more efficiently.

Swing

The swing pass is similar to the flare as the ball is thrown softly—and usually with a slight loft—in front of a running back, enabling him to take in the pass at full stride.

TEXAS PLACEKICKER Russell Erxleben demonstrates the straight-ahead style of booting field goals and extra points.

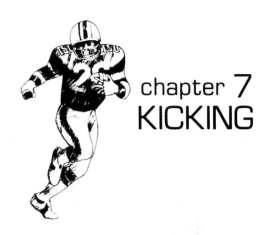

chapter 7
KICKING

USC and UCLA have staged many great battles on the gridiron, but few were as dramatic as their 1977 struggle on Nov. 25. A national television audience had witnessed a seesaw affair all evening. UCLA appeared to have the decision—and conference title—locked with a 27-26 lead, less than 2 minutes remaining, and the opponent deep in its own territory. But the Trojans started a drive, got to the Bruin 22 with just over 20 seconds left, and gambled with one more quick run to the 21 and the center of the field. Out raced Frank Jordan, the placekicker, and Mike Carey, his holder. They barely had time to get set behind the line of scrimmage before the snap. Carey grabbed the football, and put it down just before Jordan's foot came whistling through. The kick, with 2 seconds to go, was perfect. USC won 29-27 and UCLA lost the game and a trip to the Rose Bowl.

Kicking is a very important part of football, a part that is unfortunately often overlooked by coaches at the lower levels.

There are three ways to kick a football during a game: Punt, placekick, or dropkick. The dropkick is rarely used since the ball's shape has changed to favor the passing game and thereby reduced its practicality.

The punt is used as a defensive measure, usually in the offensive team's own territory when it has to relinquish possession because of failure to advance the ball the ten yards needed for a first down. Occasionally, a team will punt before fourth down in a surprise maneuver to gain better field position—especially when a game is played in rain, snow, or on a muddy field. A punt can be used for a kickoff to the opposing team after a safety has been scored.

The placekick is used for kicking off and for scoring. It must be used for the kickoff, and can be used following a safety when the ball is put in play from the 20-yard line of the team that gave up the two points. The placekick is used for

THE PUNTER lines up approximately 13 to 15 yards behind the center to take the snap.

scoring one extra point following a touchdown or for a field goal, which can be kicked from any spot on the field short of the goal line.

HOW TO PUNT

The punter should stand 13 to 15 yards behind the line of scrimmage and take the snap directly from the center. He should hold his hands stretched out in front of him to give the center a target for his snap because it is a longer distance for him than normal.

After receiving the ball, the punter should hold it in front of him with both hands—one a little farther down one side than the other—at approximately waist level. Then, he should take three forward steps, the left foot first for a right-footed punter, to quickly generate power before kicking. It is vital to move quickly before rushing defenders attempt to block the kick.

Just before the foot is planted for the last step, the football should be dropped from a spot a little lower than waist level to be met by the kicking foot as it is coming through from a pendulum-like swing.

The contact between foot and the football is the most important part of the sequence. The contact is made when the football is dropped directly onto the instep of the kicking foot. The toes should be pointing downward to ensure proper arching of the foot. The ball should be dropped on top of the arch bone, or a little to the outside.

A NORTH CAROLINA STATE punter manages to get off his kick before the charging Illinois players can block it.

The knee of the kicking foot should be bent slightly when contact is made but should be locked by the time the football leaves the foot. It is the snap of the knee from a slightly bent position to a final locked position which provides much of the power. The rest of the power is supplied by the swinging of the kicking leg.

The entire punting motion should be as fluid as possible. Unless a punt is purposely kicked to put the football out of bounds for field position or to avoid a touchback (the offensive team kicking or passing the ball into the end zone), the ideal punt is the one that travels high and far, thus allowing the punt coverers to get under it. This objective is better achieved with a smooth, well-timed punt than with one in which brute force is used.

Occasionally when a team is deep in its own territory and field position is important, a quick kick may be used. This punt is made before fourth down and not from the normal punting formation, thereby surprising the defense. The objective is to get the ball past the deep defenders to eliminate a runback and gain the best field position. The quick kick works better at the college, high school, and lower levels of play than in professional football because punters on professional teams usually are specialists who do nothing but punt, and their presence on the field would tip the defense. For the quick kick, the ball is either snapped directly to the punter who moves into position just before the play, or it is lateraled to him by another player receiving the snap.

HOW TO PLACEKICK

Even though the placekick has different objectives, kickoff, point after touch-down, and field goal, it involves the same basic motion. The main difference, however, is that the placekick for points involves accuracy—while the kickoff involves distance. All placekicking requires teamwork and when done for points involves great duress because the defense is trying to block the scoring attempt.

The placekick for points requires a maximum concentration of the three players who must touch the ball: the center, the holder, and the kicker. Their efforts have to be coordinated with the blocking of their teammates to allow enough time against onrushing defensive players. The whole sequence should take about two seconds.

The placekick for points can be broken down into three parts. It begins with the center, who snaps the football to the holder, who is on one knee with the other leg usually stretched out in front of him. The ideal snap is one that arrives at the holder, who usually is seven or eight yards behind the line of scrimmage, at chest level and directly over the spot where the ball is to be placed. The second part involves the holder. He can be any of the offensive players on the field other than the center, providing he lines up in the backfield to take the snap. Many times the quarterback is the holder because he handles the ball more than anyone else on the team besides the center.

The holder has the responsibility of placing the football on the ground for the placekicker. After taking the snap, ideally he should put the ball down in an upright position with the laces facing the goal while holding it upright with his index finger of the hand nearest the kicker's foot. The holder is on one knee to put

him closer to the kicking spot and thereby reduce the amount of time needed for the play.

The holder also has inherited one of the more thankless jobs in football, a chore that usually goes unnoticed until a mistake has been made. Paradoxically, it can be one of the most difficult jobs. The holder is the middleman in the placekicking sequence with an onrushing kicker on one side and charging defensive players on the other. He has only a split-second to recover from a bad snap, and if he judges there is not enough time for the kick, he has to either take the ball and run or pass it himself. For this emergency action, a player used to handling the ball frequently is the best insurance.

The final stage belongs to the place-kicker. He, especially at the professional and major college level, usually is a specialist who performs no other function. As a result, it is a job in which performance can be measured solely by the number of points he scores and the distances of his kicks.

The majority of football's placekickers use the straight-ahead style, approaching the football as an extension of a straight line drawn between the middle of the goal, the center, and the holder. Some placekickers use the soccer-style kick, approaching the ball and holder at an angle instead of a straight line and kicking the ball on the inside of the foot. When the straight-ahead style is used, a special kicking shoe with a square toe instead of a rounded one is recommended.

Placekicking for a field goal or extra point, the kicker should line up three normal strides behind the spot where the ball is to be placed by the holder. If the kicker is right-footed, he stands with his right foot just in front of the left. In approaching the football, he takes a step and a half, beginning just before the holder receives the football. He starts

THE PLACEKICK directly involves three offensive
players, starting with the snap from the center.

THE HOLDER fields the snap.

AFTER CATCHING the football, the holder puts it
down for the kicker.

DAN BEAVER of Illinois preferred the soccer style when it came to placekicking.

with a short step with the kicking foot to gain momentum. The next step is the power stride in which the left foot is planted in a spot about six inches behind the ball. This second step is especially important because it generates the power to give the ball distance. The kicking leg swings in an arc with the knee flexed and finishing with a snap. Right after contact, the knee joint is locked and the toe pointing upward. This aids in locking the ankle, which increases accuracy and power.

The follow-through with the kicking leg should finish at waist level, making the whole sequence resemble a half-circle. The kicker should concentrate on a follow-through in which the kicking leg is in a line perpendicular to the middle of the goalposts.

Just as in punting, timing is important in placekicking, and it can be best achieved with one fluid motion. The kicker should not try to muscle the football.

More height can be obtained by kicking lower on the football. The more the ball is scooped in this manner, however, the more distance will be sacrificed.

In kicking off to start play after a score or at the beginning of the game or second half, the kicker uses essentially the same motions as in the attempt for a field goal or extra point. The prime difference is that the kicker approaches a football that stands alone on the tee because the defense is farther away and cannot rush until the ball has been kicked. There is no center snap and holder. Because of these differences, the kicker starts from about ten yards behind the ball to generate additional power. There is no point in starting farther away—it will not increase speed or the distance of the kick. And if the kicker gets too far away, it can become difficult to coordinate the kicking motion.

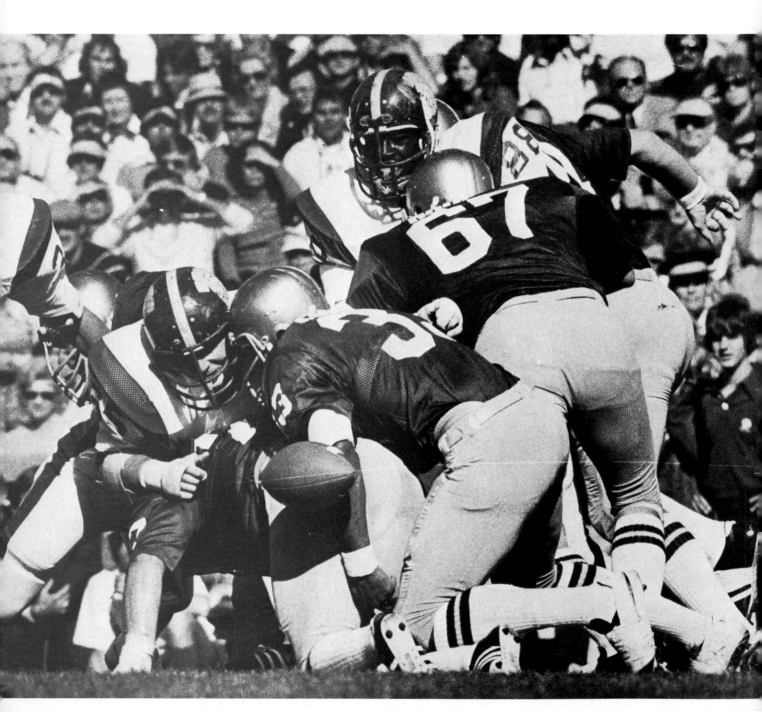

THE MICHIGAN STATE defensive line forces a Notre Dame fumble.

chapter 8
DEFENSIVE POSITIONS

Defensive linemen rarely get a chance to run with the football and, when they do, they can be excused for getting a little excited. None ever got more notoriety than California's Roy Riegel, a defensive center who scooped up a Georgia Tech fumble in the 1929 Rose Bowl and took off for the goal line. Riegel galloped 69 yards before being tackled—by a teammate! His run had been in the wrong direction. He had been spun around after grabbing the loose ball. The play led to a Georgia Tech safety and an 8–7 victory, for the Rambling Wrecks.

Each of the 11 defensive players on the field has a specific position, but they operate in three main areas: linemen, linebackers, and deep backs.

The number of players in each defensive area can vary depending on what formation the team is using, as well as what offensive action is anticipated. For instance, the line has as few as three persons in some formations (particularly in passing situations) and as many as six in others (when a run is expected). Sometimes, a defensive team will overload a specific area with players when the intentions of the offense are obvious. An example would be when a team has lined up to punt and extra players will be used to stop a blocked punt. Or, when a team is desperate for long yardage with little time remaining, extra players may be used to offset a pass rush.

As a result, the defensive player's title is not as meaningful as those on offense because there tends to be more overlap. In the line, however, there usually are ends, tackles, and guards. The middle spot, opposite the offensive center, is called nose guard. He is backed by outside and middle linebackers, who are backed by cornerbacks and safeties.

LINEMEN

The line is where the action starts for the defense, and defensive linemen have two chief objectives: Stop the opposition's

A DEFENSIVE LINEMAN demonstrates the four-point stance.

ARKANSAS DEFENSIVE TACKLE Jimmy Walker closes in on a Texas A & M quarterback.

running game and make it difficult to pass.

Because both objectives are usually best met by penetrating the opposition's line, ideal defensive linemen are players quick enough to get a good jump on the snap and strong enough to ward off blockers.

Guards

Guards play right in the center of the defensive line. Sometimes there is only one guard, the nose guard, or noseman, usually playing directly over the offensive center. Otherwise, there are left and right guards.

Guards spend most of their time trying to stop runs up the middle, which requires plenty of strength to fight off blockers in order to make a tackle. When the offense passes, the guards' job is to get through blockers forming a wall around the passer. Defensive guards, like offensive guards, start from either a three- or four-point stance.

Occasionally, guards need to watch for fakes when the offense takes advantage of the penetration and thus runs a play countering that motion, which leaves the guards with nothing to tackle. These plays are called traps.

Tackles

Defensive tackles line up just to the outside of the guard or guards. Traditionally, unlike the guards, there are almost always two tackles, left and right.

A defensive tackle's job closely resembles a guard's. Sometimes the tackle has a little more room to operate in, which means he is freer to pursue the ball and can alter his penetration routes. Tackles start from the same stances as the guards.

Ends

Two players are always responsible for guarding the flanks of the defensive line. Sometimes, though, these positions are played not by linemen but by linebackers who have been moved forward onto the line of scrimmage.

No matter where the players defending the flanks are stationed, their duty is to diagnose the play correctly before penetrating or standing ground. A mistake can result in a sizable gain for the opposition because the wrong move can take defensive ends farther away from the action where there are fewer teammates to give support, break down the offensive blocking, and bring down the ball carrier.

Strength and quickness are needed by

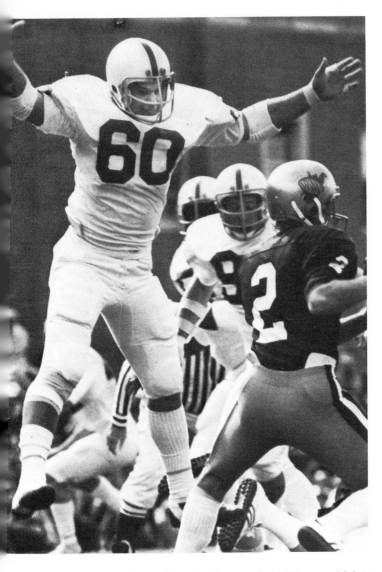

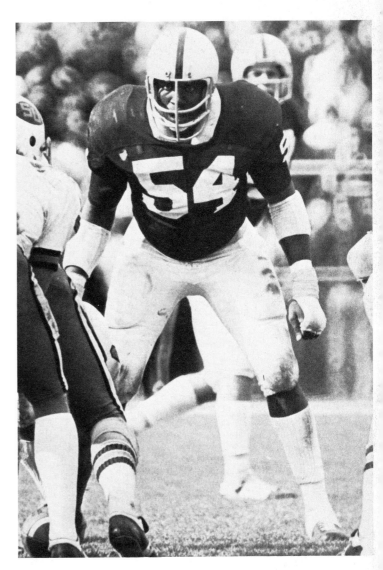

PENN STATE defensive lineman Matt Millen goes high to prevent the West Virginia quarterback from throwing a pass.

PENN STATE'S Bruce Clark shows the proper stance— as well as good concentration—for a linebacker.

defensive ends because the offense often will try to isolate the defenders with several blockers in front of the runner to achieve potentially big gains.

The defending flankers need to exercise more caution than the interior defensive linemen, but when it becomes apparent how the play is unfolding the end must make an all-out commitment.

LINEBACKERS

Some of the best athletes on a football team are linebackers because their positions require a variety of skills.

The linebackers are the middlemen in the defense, stationed between the line-

men and the deep backs. They are supposed to stop runners who get past the line in front of them before the runners can get to the backs behind them. They must have the strength to fight off blockers and make tackles in addition to having the speed to pursue runners. Sometimes they will be called on to perform the same duties as linemen, namely rush the play. Other times, their responsibilities include pass defense when they must guard against receivers—usually tight ends and running backs—in the linebacker's defensive zone.

Normally there can be as many linebackers as five in a formation and as few

HERE'S THE VIEW a cornerback has just before a play is set in motion.

as one. They can be divided into two classes.

Middle Linebacker

Middle linebacker is one of the sport's real glamour positions. It is the defensive counterpart to the quarterback on offense.

The middle linebacker lines up directly behind the center of the line facing the quarterback. His chief job is to stop runs up the middle or short passes to tight ends in his zone. After he has determined that the play will not be in his area, he then pursues the ball and helps teammates.

The middle linebacker usually calls the signals for the defense, that is, he must anticipate the offensive strategy, tell teammates their formation for the next play, and then change it at the line of scrimmage if he spots something that indicates the offensive play is not what

had been expected. The middle linebacker in his upright position only a few yards from the offense has the best vantage point for the defense.

Outside Linebackers

Outside linebackers play on the outside flank of the middle linebacker and behind their own defensive line. The duties are roughly the same as those of the middle linebacker except that it helps if the outside linebacker is a little quicker because he will have to cover more ground toward his outside flank.

DEEP BACKS

Deep backs are the last line of defense and therefore very important. A mistake here and it probably will mean a touchdown.

The prime requirement is speed. The deep backs always are matched against the offense's swiftest players. They must

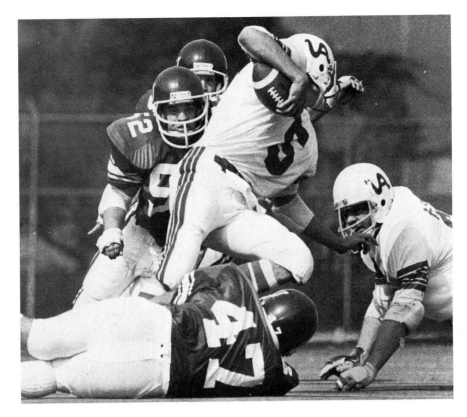

THESE NORTHWESTERN PLAYERS circle the Arizona quarterback to make the tackle.

also, however, be tough enough to bring down a strong runner who has made it through the other two lines of defense.

There are two basic positions.

Cornerback

Typically, there are two cornerbacks with the job of guarding the flanks behind the ends and outside linebackers. This position requires good lateral movement because cornerbacks move both to the outside and inside either to stop ballcarriers who have broken loose or to cover pass receivers running their routes. Cornerbacks must also coordinate their moves with teammates because vacating an area too soon may allow the defense to become victimized by a particularly deceptive play.

A cornerback plays either a zone or man-to-man defense along with the other linebackers. In the zone, he guards a specific area. In man-to-man, he guards a specific player.

Safety

The safety is often called football's center fielder because he is so far from the line of scrimmage. In effect, he is more like a utilityman because he gives help wherever it is needed.

A safety's chief duty is to watch for the pass and never let a receiver get behind him because a completion in that case most likely means a touchdown. Once the safety has determined there will be no pass, however, when the ball carrier is past the line of scrimmage, the safety moves forward to stop him.

Often there is more than one safety. In such a case, one is usually given the freedom to roam (he is called the "free safety") and the other or others are assigned a specific duty.

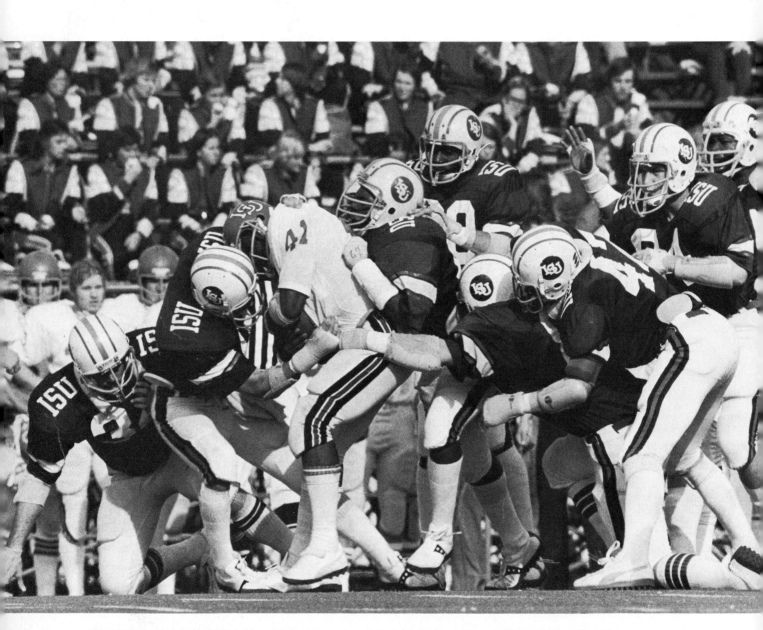

PRACTICALLY THE ENTIRE Indiana State defense gets into the act of stopping an Illinois State ball carrier.

chapter 9
TACKLING

The Detroit Lions had suffered through a disappointing season in 1962. A heartbreaking loss to Green Bay early and a loss later to the New York Giants had eliminated them from title contention. The Packers, who would go on to win the championship, appeared invincible when they came to Detroit with a 10 win-no loss record for their Thanksgiving Day rematch. But, the fired-up Lions sacked quarterback Bart Starr ten times, and he finished the game with 110 yards in losses. His running backs were dumped seven more times for losses. The furious Detroit rush produced nine points for the Lions by the time the game was only 18 minutes old. The final Detroit victory was one of the greatest displays of tackling ever seen in the NFL.

Tackling is rugged. It is, in effect, a collision between the tackler and the ball carrier.

Tackling is similar to blocking with one major exception: The tackler can use his hands and arms to stop the runner's forward progress, which is the tackler's goal.

MENTAL ATTRIBUTES

Tackling, by its very nature, demands certain mental characteristics.

At the top of the list has to be aggressiveness, for the tackler must seek out the ball carrier and stop him despite the blockers who will try to interfere. The tackler cannot wait for the runner to come to him. To do so gives the runner more momentum and consequently extra yardage.

A good tackler must concentrate and be alert. The offense's goal is to prevent the tackler from stopping the ball carrier, but the tackler may recover from a first block and have another opportunity. If the tackler is diverted, he must quickly recover and continue pursuing the play until it is over.

And, just as important as concentration, alertness, and pursuit for the tackler is poise. Because tackling is a tough,

TEXAS A & M FULLBACK George Woodard discovers it can be very difficult trying to gain yardage against the gang-tacking efforts of Texas.

physical action, the tackler must remain cool. If he doesn't, the other mental attributes that it takes to be successful will be diminished.

FUNDAMENTALS

Remember there is no such thing as a perfect tackle. Whatever is necessary to legally stop a ballcarrier is what must be done.

If a 170-pound cornerback faces a charging 240-pound fullback, obviously the tackler will want to do something to offset his size disadvantage. If a 275-pound tackle is trying to catch a swift 175-pound halfback, he will want to do something to offset his opponent's speed.

There are basic physical fundamentals to be followed, but it must also be remembered that in tackling it is the result that counts. A tackler gets no points for style.

SOMETIMES A TACKLER is forced to grab onto anything available to stop a ball carrier. This Northern Illinois defender latches onto an Indiana State player's shoulder pads.

PENN STATE LINEBACKER Ron Hostetler braces himself for a collision with the runner.

A MINNESOTA TACKLER hangs onto this Illinois runner.

Balance

The tackler must keep his balance by evenly distributing his weight on his feet and keeping his knees flexed. If the tackler overcommits his weight in any one direction, it becomes easier for the runner to get past him by taking the opposite route.

Head Up

In order to tackle a ball carrier, the tackler must see him. In order to see him, the tackler cannot let his head drop or his attention wander.

Timing

A tackler should not make his move until he is sure of tackling the ball carrier. A quick, deceptive runner can take advantage of an overeager tackler, and with one fake the runner will be gone.

When a tackler is about to make contact, he unleashes himself to get maximum power for the hit. Strength for a hard charge will come from the legs, and the tackler uses them to drive into his target. The tackler does not wait for the runner to come to him.

Leverage

The tackler must know the best spots to hit a ball carrier to bring him to the ground. If the runner is bigger and stronger than the tackler, he will want to concentrate on hitting the runner at the waist, knees, or ankles, where he is most vulnerable.

If the runner is smaller and faster, the tackler will want to make his move immediately. He does not attempt to match the player's speed. In pursuing him, the tackler looks ahead for the best angle to intersect with him.

Sight

The tackler should not follow the movements of the ball carrier's head or shoulders to determine his next move or in what direction he will be going. The head and shoulder movements are most often used to fake the tackler. Instead, the tackler concentrates on the runner's waist and legs. He has to go in the direction they take him. Sometimes it can be a good idea to watch the football, but only if it is tucked close to the carrier's body. It has to go where he goes.

TYPES OF TACKLES

Head-On

When the ball carrier is coming right at the tackler, he must concentrate on making his hit in the midsection and then on wrapping his arms around the runner to prevent escape. This is the basic tackle, and the tackler must be ready to judge quickly whether he has the strength to make it an effective hit.

In order to make this tackle effective the tackler should be bent forward with his arms spread to grasp the runner, thus preventing the runner from breaking the tackle. The tackler drives his shoulder into the runner's midsection with as much momentum as he can muster.

The tackler must be careful not to go too low to make the tackle, for the runner's legs and feet are smaller, more elusive targets, and the tackler will have only one shot. If he misses the midsection, it is always possible to grab a leg or ankle as he falls to the ground.

After making contact, the tackler should lift the ball carrier off the ground, thus causing him to lose his legs as a source of power. The tackler must keep driving after the initial hit to insure that the runner will fall backward and not forward for extra yardage.

Side Tackle

Obviously, a tackler cannot always get himself in position to make a head-on tackle. Very often he will approach the ball carrier from an angle, in which case the important requirement is good body control. He must know the exact moment and spot to drive his shoulder or other part of his body into the runner, to get maximum impact.

The tackler should make sure that his head is in front of the ball carrier, thus making it more difficult for him to get past. Also, it is vital for the tackler to get his arms wrapped around the runner because the tackler cannot always stop the runner's momentum. When the tackler approaches from the side—or at an angle—the target should be the runner's midsection. If the tackler goes higher, the runner can more easily fend off the tackle. If the tackler goes lower, there is less to grab.

High Sideline

Sometimes when the ball carrier is running next to the sideline and the tackler approaches from his side, the best approach is a high shoulder tackle. The key for the tackler here is to time his effort so that he does not miss making contact. It is not important for him to get his arms wrapped around the runner and bring him down because there is the alternative of knocking him out of bounds.

Open Field

When a ball carrier gets past the first lines of defense the tackler will likely find him-

THIS HIGH SCHOOL tackler demonstrates excellent form in hitting the ball carrier low.

THIS ILLINOIS QUARTERBACK is going nowhere: One Minnesota tackler has his legs wrapped up, another holds onto his head, and several more Gopher teammates are about to join the action.

A BALL CARRIER finds it difficult to advance when his legs have been cut from underneath him.

self in a one-on-one position with the runner in the open field. Then it is vital that the tackler make the tackle because a miss probably will result in a touchdown.

If the runner is considerably stronger than the tackler and has a good deal of steam built up by the time he reaches the tackler it may be advisable for the tackler to make a driving shoulder tackle from a slight angle to reduce the force with which he will be hitting. The tackler should stay low, however, and aim for the knees. It is more difficult for the tackler to make effective contact high because of the momentum the runner has generated.

It is not so important in this situation for the tackler to overpower the runner. The goal of an open-field tackle is just to make sure the runner is stopped or, failing that, delayed to allow time for teammates to help.

Gang Tackling

The more defensive players making the tackle, the better the chance that the runner will be stopped. Moreover, gang tackling creates a better chance that the runner will fumble the football.

If the tackler sees a teammate about to make a tackle and he is in a position to help, he should not hesitate to join the action, for the joint tackle can be especially demoralizing for the runner as well as physically punishing.

Rear Tackle

If a tackler approaches a slower moving ballcarrier from behind, he should drive his shoulder into the lower part of the runner's back and envelop him with his arms. The runner's legs will become entangled, and he will quickly come tumbling to the ground.

Sacks

To sack is the term used when the defense tackles the quarterback behind the line of scrimmage, usually while he is attempting to pass. The sack is one of the ultimate goals for a defensive player, and the number of sacks made is a statistic as important for the defensive player as yards gained or touchdowns scored are for an offensive player.

When rushing the passer, the defensive player must make his attack a controlled one. In other words, a rush with complete, reckless abandon usually does not work

A NORTH CAROLINA defender gets a hand on this ball carrier; sometimes that's all that is necessary to throw a runner off balance.

ONE TACKLER HITS this runner low and another is about to make a higher hit.

DAN HAMPTON of Arkansas (86) leads a Razorback defensive charge against Oklahoma.

A MINNESOTA RUNNING back can't make much headway carrying a tackler.

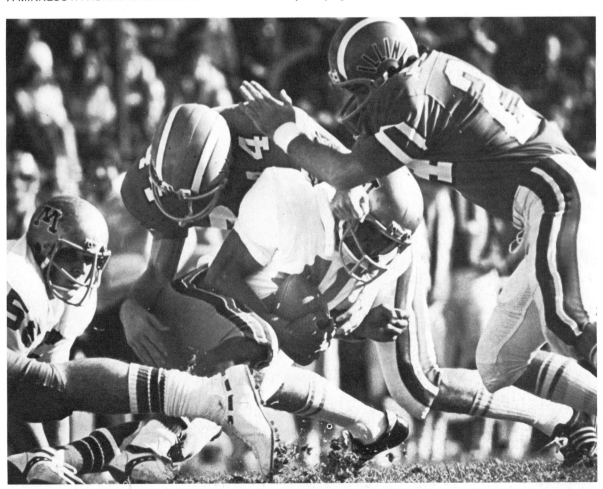

TWO COLORADO DEFENDERS lower their shoulders before making contact with an Iowa State runner.

THE GOAL FOR every tackler is to cause a fumble, and that's exactly what Ohio State's Ray Griffin does as he tackles Lonnie Perrin of Illinois.

because blockers and the quarterback will take advantage of the predictable, straight route the attacker will be taking and be able to block or evade them.

A sack usually is the result of teamwork in which the defensive linemen take predetermined routes to cut down on the space in which the quarterback has to roam while he is looking for receivers. The hit should be high, for a tackle around the legs still gives the passer a chance to get rid of the ball.

Pursuit

The defensive player should never give up once he has missed a tackle, or when the play has seemingly gone in the opposite direction. Football is a game of counters and adjustments, and it is entirely possible if the defensive player pursues that the play will come back in the defensive player's area or that he can catch up with the ball carrier because of some delay.

Fighting Off Blockers

A defensive player should not waste time with blockers. It is better for him to avoid the blocker completely and then make a quick recovery step or two to make the tackle.

It is legal for the defensive player to use his hands and arms; so the defensive player should not hesitate to simply pull or push the blocker out of his way. Sometimes, especially in sideline situations or in the middle of the line, it is possible to use the blocker to stop the ball carrier by moving him into the runner's path.

HOW TO PRACTICE

Tackling, like blocking, is not difficult to practice. All it takes is a willing teammate or dummies to serve as the target.

It is only through constant repeating of fundamentals that a defensive player will become a sure tackler. Practice does not always have to be at full speed or with equipment, but the defensive player should be sure to work at facing a variety of situations.

NO MATTER WHAT the formation, Northwestern quarterback Randy Dean discovers nothing works when the blocking breaks down.

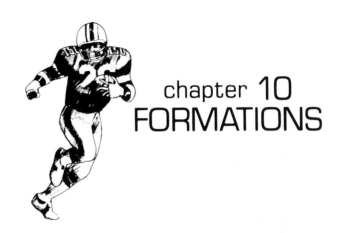

chapter 10
FORMATIONS

"We'll never forget the way you thrilled the nation with your T-formation"—refrain from Chicago Bears fight song.

How your team will line up for each down on offense or defense is as important as anything that can happen during a football contest.

It is one thing to have a squad blessed with outstanding talent, but it is still another to take full advantage of skillful players by using the right formations. Conversely, a team without exceptional talent often can enhance its effectiveness through the use of exactly the right formation.

The key to any formation is execution. There is no magic in simply lining players up in a good formation. They still have to follow their assignments.

Many coaches prefer to keep their formations and plays simple and to work hard at mastering simple tactics. Others prefer multiple approaches with a variety of formations and fancy plays. The most

important consideration is that players and alignments should complement each other. There is no sense in using a passing formation for a team blessed with plenty of good runners.

The ability to evaluate the players' skills and adapt them to the best formation is what separates the best coaches from the rest. For some, it is a matter of designing the best strategies based on available talent. For others, the approach is to fit the available players into the system.

The approach taken on defense will depend greatly on the systems employed by the opposing team's offense. Some coaches, however, are so confident of their defensive unit that they will make little compensation for the opposing team, relying on the defense's strength to stop the foe.

EVOLUTION

Many formations have been used by football teams. Some from the earliest days

COACHES OFTEN HAVE to improvise during games. Here players are shown a new formation while the contest is in progress.

THE COACH REVIEWS assignments with his players.

INDIANA STATE running back Vincent Allen was such a threat that his coach used offensive formations specifically designed to spring him free.

ONE OF THE significant developments for an offensive formation was putting a man in motion. Here, No. 45 attempts to confuse the defense by going in motion just before the snap.

are no longer used because of rule changes that have made them illegal, or because other circumstances have made them ineffective.

The introduction of the forward pass, two-platoon football, specialization, and improved speed and size have all played major roles in the formations and strategies used.

The evolution of offensive formations has been more extensive and attention-getting than that involving the defenses. In recent years, however, the defenses have come under closer scrutiny as teams and coaches have put more emphasis on stopping the opposition rather than just trying to outscore it. More and more, the better athletes are being used on defensive units which employ multiple approaches with both zone and man-to-man coverages.

The first major offensive alignment in the 1890s was the flying wedge in which nine offensive players would lock arms and form a V-formation with an additional blocker and the ballcarrier in the middle. It was popularized in 1894 by Penn coach George Woodruff, but eventually it was outlawed in 1906.

Coaches were continually tinkering in an attempt to beat their opponents. Pulling linemen for added blocking was introduced early in this century, and the idea became the basis for the famous Green Bay sweep popularized by Coach Vince Lombardi.

The forward pass was legalized in 1906, but as so often happens with new wrinkles it took well-known teams to really draw attention to this new weapon. In this case, it was Gus Dorais of Notre Dame who stunned Army with his aerials to Knute Rockne in 1913. Dorais completed 13 of 17 passes for 243 yards and a touchdown.

Passing opened up offenses as coaches worked at getting receivers open to make catches. The single wing became one popular formation. A back was stationed on the outside flank behind the scrimmage line. Next came splitting one of the ends—sometimes both—farther from the interior line.

Knute Rockne introduced the shift at Notre Dame in the 1920s. This maneuver meant that backs moved to different locations just before the snap, the purpose being to not reveal their alignment until the last second because defenses remained stationary in those days. The single wing has remained one of the popular offenses as coaches continue to use variations.

The professional teams made contributions, too. The Chicago Bears introduced the T-formation in 1931 after limited use elsewhere. This innovation was a big step forward because the quarterback moved directly behind the center to take the snap. His backs formed a straight line parallel to the scrimmage line behind him. The backs thus had more running room before taking a handoff or taking an outside route for a pass. It also meant the quarterback dropped back to pass and after it became legal in 1940 for the passer to throw from anywhere behind the line of scrimmage, the formation became more popular than ever.

Other wrinkles added were men in motion from the backfield to become deeper passing targets and the split formations, in which both backs and linemen lined up farther away from teammates to spread the defenses.

There continue to be many innovations, as coaches work at taking advantage fully of the talents of particular players.

The following are some of the basic offensive and defensive formations used today with the emphasis on the positions of the backs and receivers. The space

SPLITTING AN END apart from the rest of the line was one way of opening up the offense.

ANOTHER WAY OF opening up the offense is the use of a flankerback. Here the flanker is at the far left.

THE T-FORMATION, in which the running backs form a straight line behind the quarterback, became a major breakthrough when the quarterback lined up just behind the center to take the snap.

between the interior linemen varies according to the specific blocking objectives needed for each play.

STANDARD T

This, along with the single wing and shotgun, is the oldest of the formations that is still used today. However, use of the Standard T is found more at the high school and college levels than in professional football. It is an offensive formation that can help a running attack, for many variations of handoffs and blocking combinations can be run with so many backs close to the quarterback.

E   T   G   ⊗   G   T   E

QB

RB   RB   RB

SPLIT T

The emphasis here is on splitting the players farther apart from each other—especially in the line. This tends to open up the defenses and allow more running room for quick backs.

```
E  T  G  ⓧ  G  T  E
      QB
   RB        RB
       RB
```

WISHBONE

This is a relatively new variation of the T-formation. It also is a running formation, but it makes for quicker hits into the line with the middle running back moved a few steps closer to the line. It also extensively employs the quarterback as a fourth running back on end runs.

```
E  T  G  ⓧ  G  T  E
      QB

       RB

   RB        RB
```

POWER I

This is a running formation with the backs lined up in a straight, perpendicular formation resembling a capital letter I behind the quarterback. Plenty of blocking is provided by this formation. Teams usually use only two running backs behind the quarterback and use the other as a flanker. One of the advantages of this formation is that it is easy to disguise offensive intentions.

```
E  T  G  ⓧ  G  T  E
      QB
      RB
      RB
      RB
```

THE I-FORMATION became popular in the late 1960s. Here is the I-formation with a flanker.

SINGLE WING

With this formation, a running back is stationed behind an end. Many times another lineman, usually a tackle, also is shifted to that wing to provide extra blocking for this run-oriented alignment.

```
E  T  G  ⓧ  G  T  E
      QB        WB
  RB  RB
```

DOUBLE WING

Passing is the advantage of this formation, for two backs are placed on separate wings. Combined with the ends, they give the quarterback plenty of targets with so many players in a position to quickly get into open territory.

```
E  T  G  ⓧ  G  T  E
WB        QB        WB
       RB
```

TRIPLE WING

This is also a passing formation with three potential receivers stationed on one wing. It presents a tough problem for the defense, especially if the receivers on the wing are particularly fast. It is also a formation that lends itself to screen passes.

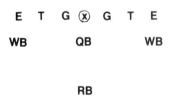

KEY TO DIAGRAMS

RB—running back	OLB—outside linebacker
WB—wing back	R—rover
FL—flanker	NG—nose guard
SB—slot back	C—cornerback
MLB—middle linebacker	S—safety

SLOT BACK

This formation features a back simply slipped into a slot between an end and tackle. It is an especially good way of providing an extra blocker on outside plays.

STANDARD PRO

This is the formation used by many pro teams, as it provides a balanced approach both for running with two backs close to the quarterback and for passing with a flanker and an end split wide.

SHOTGUN

This formation uses the old approach of snapping the football to a back several yards behind the center. The purpose is to give the player receiving the ball more room to analyze the defense. It also gives the passer more time to look for receivers because he doesn't have to backpedal.

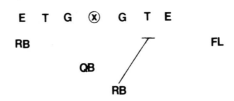

DEFENSE

Defensive formations vary according to the opponent's offense. More and more, as offenses become extremely sophisticated, coaches are spending plenty of time devising formations to stop the other teams.

The defenses have become almost as intricate as the offenses with a variety of zone and man-to-man coverages incorporated relative to what is anticipated from the team with the ball. Here are some of the basic formations used today.

6-1 DEFENSE

This defense is used frequently in high school and college games. It features six linemen, but the two ends should be quick enough to drop back as linebackers to help the lone middle linebacker. With six men on the line, the offense usually finds it tough to run against the 6-1. The remaining four defenders are cornerbacks and safeties guarding against passes and runners making it through the front wall.

```
    E  T  G     G  T  E
          MLB
 CB                    CB


      S         S
```

4-3 DEFENSE

This standard defense used by many professional teams features a four-man line and three linebackers. The linebackers are stationed so that they can go forward to stop the run or easily drop back to defend against a pass, making it a well-balanced alignment.

```
      E   T     T   E
     OLB    MLB    OLB


       CB         CB


          S     S
```

THE 4-3 DEFENSE is the formation used by many professional teams.

4-4 DEFENSE

This defense is used by many top college teams, especially against teams not so likely to throw the long pass. With four linebackers, the offense usually finds it difficult to block the defenders with so much congestion on short pass and running situations.

```
      E   T     T   E
     LB  LB     LB  LB


       CB         CB


           S
```

5-2 DEFENSE

The feature here is a linebacker who is free to roam and follow the ball. He is called the roverback or monster, lining up against the strong side of the offense. Offenses usually find it difficult to pass against the 5-2 because the rover is in position to also drop back and aid the remaining four defenders at cornerback and safety positions.

```
    E  T  NG  T  E
        LB    LB


   CB      R      CB


          S
```

3-5 DEFENSE

This new defense is starting to be used by many professional teams with interior linemen strong enough to need only three for a pass rush. With five linebackers, though, the defense always has the option of sending an extra rusher or two. The linebackers serve as ends and also drop back to cover on passes. The key to this defense is having linebackers quick enough to cover plenty of ground.

```
       T   NG   T
      LB  LB  LB  LB  LB


       CB          CB


            S
```

THE TEAR-AWAY jersey has helped many runners pick up extra yardage.

chapter 11
EQUIPMENT

The Chicago Bears had whipped the New York Giants in two previous encounters during the 1934 season and they didn't figure to have much trouble when they met a third time for the NFL championship Dec. 9 in the Polo Grounds. The field was like an ice-skating rink because of the freezing temperatures, but the Bears still built an early lead. In the second half, though New York Coach Steve Owen introduced a secret weapon: He had his players put on basketball sneakers. Borrowed from the Manhattan College team, the sneakers provided better traction for the Giants, and with the improved footing the Giants blitzed the Bears with 27 points in the fourth quarter for a 30–13 victory.

Football is a rugged sport with almost constant body contact, often between opposing players running at full speed. For this reason, the right kind of equipment is the only security against serious injury.

Because of the possibility of injury, it is essential that equipment used be safe and in good repair. Poor quality equipment can be as dangerous as a blindside tackle.

Equipment breaks down as follows:

HELMET

Without a doubt, the helmet is the most important piece of equipment for a football player. Ask any professional and he'll tell you it would be the last item he would relinquish.

The purpose of a helmet is to protect the head from blows. Made of hard plastic, the helmet's interior, which must offer some sort of cushion to absorb a shock, is one of two types: suspension or sponge-padded.

The sponge-padded helmet protects the head directly because it is in contact with the padding inside the helmet. The suspension type offers absorption of shock through a network of straps encircling the skull.

Helmet sizes are determined in the same manner as hat sizes. The helmet

HARD-SPONGE helmet.

THE FACEMASK is a vital piece of equipment.

should fit so that the earholes are right over the ears. The fit should be snug enough so that the helmet will not move by rotating or slipping on the head. Finally, make sure that the front of the helmet does not come closer than a half-inch above the eyebrows and that the back of it does not cut into the neck when the head is tilted backward.

FACEMASK

For many players, especially those in the line where there is body contact on every play, the helmet is almost useless without a facemask. All players wear one because it offers protection for the eyes, nose, and mouth.

The facemasks, made of either metal or hard plastic, vary in styles and the amount of protection they provide. Linemen usually prefer the "birdcage" type in which three bars run horizontally across the face connected by a centered vertical bar.

Players whose positions call for them to play mainly in open spaces, such as defensive backs and wide receivers, usu-

ally prefer fewer bars on their mask. Such players need total visibility and have relatively less body contact.

CHINSTRAP

The helmet, with its facemask, can be rendered totally useless, of course, if it's knocked off. The chinstrap, a piece of leather with snaps at each end connecting both ear flaps, keeps the helmet on the head. The strap passes below the chin and should be fastened tightly enough to keep the helmet from slipping.

MOUTHPIECE

The mouthpiece, often overlooked by the player, should be fitted by the team physician or a dentist. It is a small piece of plastic which fits over the upper teeth (some mouthpieces cover lower teeth as well) and offers protection from a blow to the jaw or mouth by an opponent's elbow or knee.

SHOULDER PADS

The most important piece of equipment for the upper body is shoulder pads.

These vary in size and weight (linemen usually wear bigger and heavier pads than backfield players and ends) to allow for freedom of movement.

Essentially, shoulder pads are layers of hard plastic or rubber reinforced with webbing and steel bands. They are attached to a central collar which is draped around the neck.

These pads absorb the blows to the shoulders so common in a game that involves blocking and tackling. Pads are measured as extra large, large, medium, and small.

Proper fitting of shoulder pads requires that they come far enough down the chest so that they cover the pectoral muscles. The opening at the neck should be large enough so that there is no pinching when the arms are lifted.

FOREARM PADS

Forearm pads protect the wrists and forearms, which are always particularly vulnerable to injury for linemen. There are two basic styles: a hard plastic pad set

FOREARM PADS protect the wrists and forearms.

SHOULDER PADS prevent many injuries.

in an elastic fabric which slips right over the forearms, and the hard sponge pad with a fibrous material allowing them to be shaped and attached by the player for a natural fit.

HIP PADS

A painful but not particularly serious injury, the hip pointer can be avoided with proper padding. There are two basic forms of hip pads: the girdle, a padded pair of elastic trunks; and the strap, which wraps around the waist and buckles in front.

THIGH PADS

Thigh pads are usually pieces of plastic and foam which are slipped into special pockets in the pants. They also can be taped to the thighs to prevent slippage while in action.

RIB PADS

High school and college players usually wear rib pads. Some athletes merely tape pieces of sponge pads to their rib areas for protection. A harness is also available in which the pads are attached to the rib area by a network of suspenders.

KNEE PADS

Of all football injuries, those to the knee are the most serious. More potentially bright careers have ended prematurely because of a knee injury than any other. The knees, probably the most vulnerable area while playing football, are difficult to protect. The only means developed thus far are hard sponge rubber pads which are fitted into special pockets built into the pants similar to those for thigh pads.

SHIN PADS

Shin pads are not so common as other pads. Usually they are thin pieces of hard plastic taped to shins.

SHOES

The proper fit in shoes is important in any sport, but it is doubly so in football because the playing surface competed on may differ depending on weather and whether it is an artificial surface.

Just as with shoulder pads and helmets, a good fit is most important. Shoes—the best are made of kangaroo hide—should be snug but not so tight that blisters may develop. A player should never buy shoes a size or two too large thinking that he'll

THIS PLAYER is fully protected. Notice the thigh and knee pads.

LOW-CUT SHOES, the model preferred by most players, have cleats made of hard rubber.

grow into them. Shoes that are too large lead to poor traction and possible injury.

Almost all players today wear low cut shoes, the tops coming to the lower region of the ankles. This type of shoe allows more freedom in lateral movements. However, some players—and coaches—still prefer the older-fashioned high-top shoes, which come higher up the ankle and create more protection against sprains.

The cleats on the soles of standard football shoes usually are a half-inch to three-quarters of an inch long and made of hard rubber, providing plenty of traction for quick starts and turns. Metal cleats are illegal.

For play on artificial turf, cleats should be shorter because they will not sink into the artificial surface and it is easier for the wearer to lose balance with longer ones.

PANTS

Look at any picture of a football game played more than 30 years ago and one played today, and one of the first things you'll notice is how much more streamlined the modern uniforms appear. One of the main reasons is that pants now are made of tight-fitting synthetic materials which, in some cases, make it more difficult for a tackler to hold on to a fleeing ballcarrier. Pants today are also lighter than the baggy models of yesteryear and allow more freedom of movement.

JERSEYS

Just as tight-fitting pants make it tougher to tackle ballcarriers, tear-away jerseys which come apart with the least amount of resistance also have become popular, mostly in college football. Some jerseys also are perforated to allow better ventilation for heavy perspiration. It is advisable to wear a T-shirt underneath the jersey to prevent scratches from some of the other equipment.

TAPE

The taping of ankles and hands is so prevalent among today's football players that it can be considered almost an extension of the uniform. All professional players—and most college players—tape their ankles heavily for protection against sprains. Linemen and linebackers frequently tape their hands to guard against injuries to their fingers and knuckles.

ILLEGAL EQUIPMENT

Just as there is prescribed equipment for football players, there are also rules governing what constitutes illegal equipment. For instance, it is against the rules to wear leather or other unyielding substances on hands, wrists, or elbows—no matter how it is covered—because of the possibility of injuring an opponent. Some other examples: The jerseys of the two teams should be of contrasting colors, and neither should come close to resembling the color of the football; it is illegal to have grease or any other slippery substance on the body or uniform.

THE TEXAS CHRISTIAN player wears the type of facemask preferred by backs, while the onrushing Texas player has the type worn by most linemen.

BEING IN GOOD physical condition is one way to avoid injury.

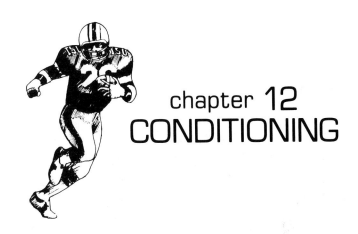

chapter 12
CONDITIONING

"The teams that win consistently are the ones in the best physical condition."—Paul (Bear) Bryant, Alabama coach.

A major cause of football injuries is improper conditioning. A football player must be in top shape to avoid injury as well as to play the game properly. Physical conditioning is often reflected in a player's ability and longevity.

A program of proper conditioning for football should include exercises designed to increase strength, speed, agility, flexibility, balance, endurance, coordination, and courage.

There are two basic ways to strengthen the body. One is through the use of elaborate weight machine programs. The other is by using an isometric exercise program, which is readily available because the player does not need expensive equipment; two people can work together to strengthen the body.

Ideally, conditioning should begin in the off-season and continue during the season. A player should work to strengthen his neck, shoulders, back, and legs during the off-season. Strength exercises should be done in all preseason, regular season, and off-season workouts. No one can be too strong to play football.

Football is a game of many, many short sprints with very little rest in between plays, so heart and lungs (cardiovascular system) must be in excellent condition.

OFF-SEASON CONDITIONING

Flexibility in the back, legs, chest, and shoulders is a must for football players. The lower back muscles and upper leg (hamstring) muscles should be loose and stretched. A player should be able to place his palms flat on the floor with his knees kept straight and feet together.

Sprinting is the best way to gain cardiovascular endurance for football. Some coaches have players run a mile or more each day in their preseason conditioning. The long distance run doesn't

PLAYERS DO NOT need expensive equipment for warm-ups. It just takes a teammate.

FOOTBALL PLAYERS should loosen their muscles before each practice and each game.

always get the player ready for the repeated short sprints needed in a football game. Repeated short sprints, just like those in a game, are needed to build the type of cardiovascular endurance needed to play football. Running a mile is fine provided many, many short sprints are run along with the mile.

Because conditioning is a year-round activity, work should begin at the close of the season. Handball, tennis, badminton, paddle tennis, swimming, and golf are all excellent conditioning activities.

Three exercise programs can be used during the off-season to build up heart and lungs and stamina. All can be done indoors with a minimum of equipment.

For the Brouca Step Test or the Harvard Step Test, all that is needed is a box or stool 20 inches high, 20 inches wide, and 20 inches deep. Step up on and down from the box 30 times a minute for five minutes. On the count of one, step up on the box with the left foot; step up with the right foot on the count of two; then step down with the left foot; and on the count of four, step down with the right foot. After two and a half minutes, change and lead with the right foot. As this exercise becomes easy, weight may be added to the feet, a weighted belt worn, or dumbbells held in each hand.

Another cardiovascular exercise for developing endurance is the Carlson Fatigue Test, which consists of running in place as fast as possible for ten seconds, resting ten seconds, and repeating the run-rest sequence ten times. Count each time the right foot makes contact with the floor and record this number after each ten second run.

Pulse rate should be checked after doing these two exercises. A quick return to normal pulse rate after exercise and an increase in the number of times the right foot hits the floor gives an indication of improvement in conditioning.

Rope skipping is another good cardiovascular exercise. Skipping rope can be done many ways—alternating on one foot and then the other foot, on both feet, or using the boxer's shuffle, in which the jump is only high enough for the rope to clear the feet. Skip rope for one minute and rest for one minute. The sequence should be repeated for ten one-minute periods with one minute of rest between. Increase repetitions as the drill becomes easier.

STRENGTH EXERCISES

In the off-season, preseason, and regular season, all players should work on exercises to maintain their strength.

Pull-Ups

Pull-ups should be done on a bar with different grips, the palms away from the body and the palms toward the body. A pull-up drill to be completed in 36 seconds should be done in the following manner: (a) pull-up flexing the elbows about 15 degrees and hold for six seconds; (b) pull-up flexing the elbows to 90 degrees and hold for six seconds; (c) pull-up looking over the bar and hold for six seconds; (d) lower slowly to 90 degrees of elbow flexion and hold for six seconds; (e) lower slowly to 15 degrees of elbow flexion and hold six seconds; (f) lower to complete elbow extension and hold stretching for six seconds. At least three 36-second pull-up exercises a day and at least ten to 20 regular pull-ups should be done daily.

Push-Ups

Push-ups should be done daily to improve and maintain shoulder, arm, and chest strength. Push-ups may be done in several ways: lying prone with hands close together with fingers and thumbs forming a triangle under the chest, with hands wide outside the shoulders, or with hands directly under the shoulders.

Try at least 15 to 25 push-ups daily, plus 36-second push-ups, stopping at different spots and holding for six seconds as was done in pull-ups. Many football players do their push-ups on their finger tips to strengthen fingers and wrists.

WARM-UP EXERCISES

Before any workout begins, all football

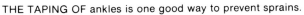

THE TAPING OF ankles is one good way to prevent sprains.

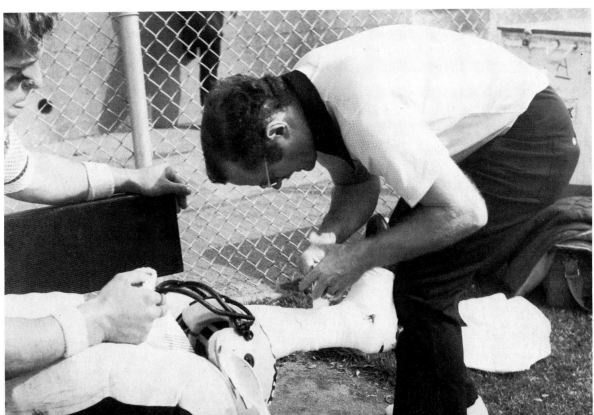

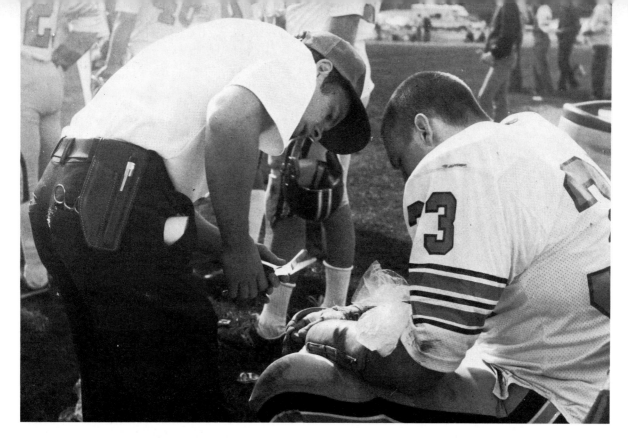

SOME INJURIES NEED only minor attention before the player is back in the game.

players should do some warm-up and stretching exercises to get the muscles and body ready. The amount or type of warm-up necessary is an individual matter, but a player should be sure he is warm and loose for a game to avoid injury.

After warm-up exercises, it is a good idea for all football players to know how to do forward and backward rolls on the ground. Players should learn how to roll and get up and jump over another player, how to do a forward roll on the left or right shoulder, and how to just duck the head and do a forward roll. He should repeat this drill until he can run, dive, and roll at full speed without hitting the ground too hard.

Agility will save many shoulder separations and contusions.

ISOMETRIC EXERCISES

Isometric exercise is a fast method for football players to gain and maintain strength. In isometric exercise, a partner resists the movement, or the exercise is done against an immovable object.

No equipment is needed to do isometric exercises, and not many repetitions are needed. Three six-second contractions at different points along the range is enough to gain—or maintain—strength. Work should be done to build up the parts of the body that are the weakest.

Before beginning an isometric exercise program, a player should always spend at least ten minutes with warm-up and stretching exercises. Choose the isometric exercises according to needs or weaknesses. It is not necessary to feel pain. If you do, ease the amount of pressure used to push against the immovable object.

FINGER AND HAND EXERCISES

Strong hands are an asset in almost all sports. Simply playing the game will not give you strong hands, and many injuries can be prevented if the hand muscles and fingers are strengthened.

All football players should have a hand

exerciser and use it frequently. A special exerciser can be purchased at most sporting goods stores, or a rubber ball may be used. By simply squeezing it, you can develop fully the hand and fingers.

It is especially important to strengthen the muscles around the joints—knees, elbows, and ankles, spots most vulnerable to injuries. Building these muscles can help to prevent many injuries.

PRE-SEASON CONDITIONING

Sprinting is an important way to condition for playing football because football is a game with so many short sprints and very little rest. If possible, do all sprinting in football shoes to toughen the feet and also to get used to the shoes. All starts should be from offensive or defensive stances. A player should not do all his sprinting straight ahead. Very few sprints in a football game will go that way for more than 15 yards. Practice sprints as they will be done in the game, cutting to the right and left. A player should sprint backwards and laterally if he is a defensive back. Sprint conditioning varies a little for each position.

REGULAR SEASON CONDITIONING

Coaches want strong football players, and so they add strength exercises to their daily programs. Ten minutes of vigorous warm-up and stretching exercises should be followed by ten to 20 minutes of strength exercises. Certain parts of the body require special attention in conditioning: the neck, shoulders, chest, stomach, back, thighs, knees, and ankles.

Fifteen to 20 minutes of each daily program should be devoted to strength-isometric exercise to produce much stronger players and fewer injuries. A player should continue isometric exercises daily on his own to strengthen weaknesses and to rebuild sprains, strains, or contusions until they have disappeared. The day after a game the injured athletes should begin isometric exercises following any necessary treatment.

Coaches usually have a regular, formal warm-up with stretching exercises (such as jumping jacks or belly-flops) before a game. They also have their own favorite drills for the lineman and backs. Warm-up and stretching, however, is an individual matter. Some players need more than others.

Warm-ups before the game begins should build up a good sweat. Coaches should be sure to allow enough time for players to get loose before the start of the second half, too.

During the game, a big problem may be how to stay warm if the temperature is low. It is important to keep the body warm on the sidelines. Running in place in front of the bench every few minutes is an effective way. Dressing warmly is another means of preventing the cold air from stiffening the body.

DIET

Each player should eat the right foods to stay in reasonably good condition. The football player who needs to add weight should be on a high protein-carbohydrate diet and continually exercise to gain strength and girth. The heavy football player should watch his calories and do resistive exercise continually to gain or maintain his strength and girth, too.

AN IMPORTANT JOB for a linesman is determining exactly where forward progress came to a halt.

chapter 13
OFFICIATING

"I told my nine-year old son after a game that I didn't take booing personally and I didn't want him to take it personally, either. He said: 'Wait a minute. I was booing, too. You blew that call. I do take it personally.' From then on, he bought his own ticket."—Norm Schachter, former NFL referee

Every sport has its rules and every sport has someone who must enforce them. It is, in many cases, a thankless but totally necessary job.

The most an official can hope for in football after making a call is silence. If the infraction is against the home team, it is almost certain that the official will get an unfavorable response from the crowd.

Officiating is as complex as playing the game. Not only are officials expected to know all the rules, they also have to make the same split-second decisions in making their calls as players do in playing the game.

Officiating also requires teamwork. In most football games that are televised, an officiating crew consists of six persons, all of whom must function smoothly together as a play develops and the action flows. Many times crews are kept together for an entire season to keep them efficient.

The officials are most noticeable to spectators and players when they take any one of the following actions: Blow a whistle to signal that a play is over; drop their flag to indicate a violation; or give a signal to indicate a call.

In the professional ranks, the crews consist of seven persons, the seventh having been added in NFL 1978 rule changes, and a reserve in case of an injury. Crews become smaller and officials assume more responsibilities, however, all the way down to kid's leagues, where often only two persons enforce the rules.

The titles and responsibilities for a seven-person crew follow. The duties may vary slightly for college officials, but the titles are the same.

THE REFEREES always try to get close to the play, to observe any infractions.

REFEREE

The referee has control and general oversight of the game, assuming final authority when there is disagreement. Occasionally, this person is forced to make a final decision that is not covered by the rules, such as calling a game off because of weather or other extenuating circumstances.

Among other duties, the referee tosses the coin to determine offensive and defensive choices and field direction before the game; signals for the football to be put in play before a kickoff; notifies coaches of remaining time left in the game, including the two-minute warning near the close of each half; administers the penalty for any infraction that is called; conducts measurements for first down; and rules on

extra-point kicks. At the start of a down play, the referee stands behind the offensive backfield and is primarily responsible for action involving the quarterback.

UMPIRE

The umpire stands behind the defensive line and usually must shift quickly to avoid getting in the way as the play develops. Among his chief responsibilities are decisions on the legality of equipment and conduct of players at the line of scrimmage.

The umpire also records the number of timeouts for each team. Among other duties, he records the results of the coin toss; keeps a dry football in play when necessary; watches for ineligible linemen downfield on a pass play; keeps an ear

HERE A LINESMAN closely follows the play.

out for attempts by the defense to simulate starting signals by the offense; and checks the legality of blocks at the scrimmage line.

HEAD LINESMAN

The head linesman takes a position on the line of scrimmage, keeping far enough away not to impede play. His chief responsibility is to watch for encroachment, known as offsides, by either the offense or defense. He also is responsible for the chain crew on the sideline who keep the measurements for first downs.

The head linesman also patrols the sidelines to determine when players are out-of-bounds, checks action among players at his end of the scrimmage line, follows any ball carrier who comes into his zone, checks for eligible receivers on pass plays, spots forward progress of the ball for the referee, and communicates the down to the referee.

LINE JUDGE

The line judge places himself at the scrimmage line on the opposite side of the field from the head linesman, checks for encroachment on his side, and observes all motion in the offensive backfield.

The line judge also keeps time whenever the field clock malfunctions, fires a pistol at the close of each period, times intermission between halves, observes the nearest sideline area, checks the action of players outside the umpire's vision, and watches for passes thrown from in front of the scrimmage line.

BACK JUDGE

The back judge operates on the same side of the field as the line judge, but about 15 yards deeper behind the defensive unit. The chief responsibility of the back judge is to observe play between receivers and defenders in ruling on passes in his area.

Among other duties the back judge counts the defensive players on the field, rules on deep passes, watches an upright opposite the one watched by the field judge on field-goal attempts, has responsibility for ruling on sideline decisions from approximately 15 yards past the scrimmage line to the end lines, watches all eligible receivers nearest him, and helps rule on passes that may have been trapped or not caught by a receiver.

FIELD JUDGE

The field judge also stands approximately 15 yards beyond the scrimmage line on the defensive side, but on the opposite side of the defensive backfield from the back judge's position. The chief responsibility of the field judge is never to let a player get behind him, for he is in charge of the field's end line.

The field judge also is responsible for timing the offense in its execution of a play (the NFL has a 30 second limit; the high school and NCAA time limit is 25 seconds) and he also times the timeouts. Other duties include observing all deep pass plays; covering the upright opposite the back judge on a field-goal try; responsibility for actions by punt receivers; and assisting the head linesman in control of a play unfolding on the same side of the field.

SIDE JUDGE

NFL 1978 rule changes created a new seventh official for professional games, the side judge. Positioned so that he can observe action formerly out of the sight lines of the other six officials, the side judge will have the responsibility of watching for the bumping of pass receivers within 5 yards beyond the line of scrimmage, but not beyond.

SIGNALS

The following are signals for many of the infractions that occur during a game.

Code of Official Signals

Touchdown or
Field Goal

Helping the Runner,
or Interlocked
Interference

Ball Ready for Play

Grasping
Face Mask

Delay of Game

Roughing the Kicker

Ball Dead; If Hand
is Moved from Side
to Side: Touchback

Illegally Passing
or Handling Ball
Forward

Incomplete Forward Pass,
Penalty Declined,
No Play, or No Score

Touching a Forward
Pass or Scrimmage Kick

Safety

Non-contact Fouls

Loss of Down

Substitution
Infractions

Clipping

Illegal Procedure
or Position

Blocking Below
the Waist

Offside (Infraction
of scrimmage or
free kick formation)

Illegal Shift

Player Disqualified

Illegal use of
Hands and Arms

Illegal Motion

Personal Foul

First Down

Ineligible Receiver
Down Field on Pass

Ball Illegally Touched,
Kicked, or Batted

Time out; Referee's
Discretionary or Excess
Time Out followed with
tapping hands on chest.

Forward Pass or
Kick Catching
Interference

Start the Clock

Intentional
Grounding

STATISTICS and outcomes are closely related.

chapter 14
STATISTICS

"Statistics are for losers."—Anonymous

Coaches love to say that the only statistic with any real meaning is the final score. That's true, of course, but nevertheless all statistics can serve a vital function.

In football, they are followed as religiously as they are in any other sport. Statistics can be particularly helpful for a coach because it is through them that he can evaluate performances of the players. For instance, he may want to make play selection in a specific game situation based on past performances that have been charted. Or, he may want to select starters on the basis of individual accomplishments—or deficiencies—as reflected in statistics.

A coach needs to have both team and individual statistics kept for each game and totaled for the season. Here are some of the more important statistics.

RUNNING

Number of rushes, total yards gained, average per rush, longest gain, fumbles, touchdowns, and penalties.

PASSING

Number of passes attempted, passes completed, passes intercepted by opponents, total yards gained, longest gain, and touchdowns. Statistics should be kept for both passers and receivers.

KICKING

Number of punts, distance, number of returns by opponents, return yardage by opponents, punts blocked by opponents, field goal attempts, field goal conversions, field goal attempts by distance from the uprights, extra point attempts, and place-kick attempts blocked.

DEFENSE

Number of tackles, tackling assists, fumbles caused, fumbles recovered, passes blocked, intereceptions, sacks, and blocked kicks. Statistics should be kept for individual players and totaled.

OTHERS

Kickoff return yardage, punt return yardage, total return yardage, number of offensive plays, opponent's plays, scoring, and penalties.

Statistics are not only for coaches and players. Many fans, and others who observe the game closely such as sportswriters and gamblers, follow them religiously, too. A 1,000-yard per season rusher on a losing team creates more excitement than the team itself.

The media often devote much time and space to statistics. In fact, the report of any game in the newspaper usually is not considered complete unless accompanied by a statistical account. Generally, it includes how and when the scoring occurred, a yardage breakdown, penalties, fumbles, location of the game, and attendance.

Notice the accompanying summary of a professional game between the Los Angeles Rams and Atlanta Falcons played in Atlanta. It starts with a score by quarters before telling you how the scoring occurred. Next comes the scoring and yardage breakdown, fumbles, and penalties—and many times this is as much as will be printed. But in this case, the account also includes individual performances.

LOS ANGELES 30, ATLANTA 14

Atlanta-Fulton County Stadium, 53,607

| Los Angeles | 0 | 6 | 7 | 17–30 |
| Atlanta | 0 | 7 | 0 | 7–14 |

Atl.—Bartkowski 1 run (Mike-Mayer kick)

L. A.—H. Jackson 19 pass from Jaworski (kick failed)
L. A.—Jaworski 1 run (Dempsey kick)
L. A.—Jessie 47 pass from Haden (Dempsey kick)
L. A.—Dempsey FG 25
Atl.—Bean 50 pass from Bartkowski (Mike-Mayer kick)
L. A.—M. Jackson 46 interception return (Dempsey kick)

	Falcons	Rams
First downs	12	17
Net yards gained	210	369
Rushing yardage	62	232
Passing yardage	148	137
Passes—Comp.—had int.	33–16–3	16–8–1
Punts	9–47.6	7–43.9
Fumbles—lost	3–1	3–3
Penalties	7–70	7–59

Rushing

Falcons—Stanback 5 for 29; Hampton 11 for 24; Bean 2 for 11; Thompson 1 for 4; Bartkowski 3 for –6.

Rams—McCutcheon 26 for 115; Cappelletti 22 for 102; Jaworski 2 for 15, 1 TD; Haden 1 for 0.

Passing

Falcons—Bartkowski 16 of 33 for 193, 1 TD.

Rams—Jaworski 7 of 15 for 90, 1 TD; Haden 1 of 1 for 47, 1 TD.

Receiving

Falcons—Thompson 4 for 21; Bean 3 for 61, 1 TD; Mitchell 3 for 35; Stanback 3 for 8; Jenkins 2 for 55; Gilliam 1 for 13.

Rams—H. Jackson 3 for 54, 1 TD; Jessie 2 for 71, 1 TD; McCutcheon 2 for 15; Cappelletti 1 for –3.

glossary

Football has a special language and it will help you to better understand the game when you know the meaning of the words used by the players, coaches, media, and knowledgeable fans

Audibles: Vocal signals by the quarterback changing a play at the line of scrimmage

Artificial Turf: The synthetic surface used on playing field in many stadiums

Backfield: The part of a team that plays behind the line of scrimmage: the quarterback and three running and/or blocking backs

Backpedal: The act of running backward to gain a better vantage point, most commonly used by quarterbacks and defensive backs

Ballcarrier: Any player with the football in his possession

Blindsided: A person being tackled from behind or on a side not watched by someone he does not see

Blitz: When linebackers or other defensive backs leave their normal positions to rush the quarterback behind the line of scrimmage. Also called red dog.

Block: Obstruction by an offensive player of a defensive player to prevent his making a tackle

Bootleg: When a quarterback hides the football along his leg after a fake handoff while moving laterally to a spot to pass or to continue with a run

Center: The offensive lineman in the middle who starts every play by passing the football through his legs to a back

Charge: The initial movement by a football player toward his objective

Completion: A pass that has been successfully received

Conversion: Try after touchdown by a kick for an extra point or a run or pass for two points

Corner: The furthest outside positions maintained by a defensive back

Cornerback: The player who defends the outside flanks of the defensive backfield

Cross: A pass pattern in which two receivers pass across each other's path on their routes

Cross Body: A block by an offensive player in which he uses his body in a horizontal position to obstruct the defensive player

Curl: A pass pattern in which the receiver runs upfield 10 to 15 yards before swinging back toward his scrimmage line to receive a pass

Cutback: When a ballcarrier changes directions

Deep Back: A defensive player who stations himself behind linemen and line-backers

Double-Teaming: When two players attempt to force one opponent into a specific course of action

Down: One scrimmage play

Downfield: The area beyond the scrimmage line

Draw Play: A running play in which the ballcarrier starts late into the line after deception is supposed to convince the defense that the play is a pass

End: A player at the flank of the scrimmage line

End Zone: The 10-yard area beyond the goal lines entrance into which by a ball-carrier or successful pass receiver constitutes a touchdown

Extra Point: The scoring done after a touchdown. In pro football, the offensive team starts from the 2-yard line and gets 1 point for either passing or running the ball past the goal line, or by kicking it through the goalposts. In college and high school, a team gets 2 points for running or passing it over the goal line and 1 for a kick.

Facemask: The padded metal bars connected to his helmet worn over a player's face

Fake: A movement intended to fool an opponent

Field Goal: Kicking the ball through the uprights with a placekick for a three-point score

Flanker: The member of the backfield who lines up wide, ostensibly to receive a pass

Fly: A pass pattern in which the receiver simply tries to get behind and outrun defenders

Forward Pass: When the football is thrown toward an opponent's goal from a spot behind the line of scrimmage

Formation: An alignment, offensive or defensive, that a team assumes before the football is snapped to set the play in motion

Fullback: A person who plays in the offensive backfield and who usually is charged with power running duties and blocking

Fumble: The loss of possession of the football by a player

Goal Lines: The lines at either end of the field that form the inside boundary of the end zone; a team scores a touchdown when it advances the football over the goal line

Goalposts: The H-shaped configuration at both ends of the field used for scoring field goals and extra points

Halfback: A member of the backfield who runs, blocks, and receives passes

Handoff: The act of giving the football directly to a teammate with an under-handed motion

Hash Marks: The chalk marks on the inbounds lines that measure off the distance between goal lines yard-by-yard. The distance they are set from the outside boundaries differs in pro and college football, but in each case when a play is out of bounds or between the inbounds line and the out-of-bounds line, the referee spots the ball on the appropriate hash mark to set the next play in motion.

Hook: A pass pattern in which a receiver runs upfield, stops, and turns to face the line of scrimmage to receive the pass

Huddle: The gathering of the team on the field into a consolidated group for the purpose of planmaking

Incompletion: A pass that was not caught by either team

Interception: A pass that was caught by the defense
Interference: When a defensive or offensive player makes illegal bodily contact with his opposite number
Kickoff: A free placekick (from the 35-yard line in pro ball and 40 in college) that starts a game, the second half, and puts the ball in play following a touchdown or field goal
Lateral: A pass to the side, often thrown underhanded
Linebacker: Defensive players positioned just behind the front line
Lineman: A player, either on offense or defense, who is stationed on the line of scrimmage at the start of each play
Line of Scrimmage: An imaginary line running through the football and perpendicular to the sideline; the offensive and defensive teams are stationed on opposite sides at the beginning of each play.
Middle Guard: A defensive lineman stationed directly in front of the offensive center. Also called nose guard.
Mouthpiece: A piece of molded rubber that fits over the upper or upper and lower teeth to help prevent injury
Offsides: When a player crosses the line of scrimmage before the ball is snapped
Off Tackle: An offensive play in which the ballcarrier tries to run through the line at the tackle spot
Pass: Throwing the football
Pattern: A predetermined route run by pass receivers
Penalty: When a team violates a rule, it usually is penalized by the ball being moved toward the goal it is defending
Pitchout: A backward toss of the ball by a member of the backfield to another member or an end
Pocket: The protective wall formed by backfield players and linemen around an offensive player attempting to pass
Post: A passing pattern in which the receiver runs to the outside and cuts diagonally toward the opponent's goalpost
Punt: The act of kicking the ball before it hits the ground
Primary Receiver: The No. 1 target of the passer
Quarterback: The offensive leader or signal-caller who usually starts each play by taking the snap from center
Receiver: A player eligible to catch a pass
Reverse: The changing of direction of an offensive play in a preconceived manner designed to confuse the defense
Roll-Out: A pass thrown after the passer moves to either his left or right side
Running Back: A member of the offensive backfield who carries the football on running plays
Rush: This can have two meanings. On offense, it means a running play. On defense, it is the charge at the snap to stop the play.
Safety: A deep back on the defensive team. Also means a score of two points awarded to the defensive team for tackling a ballcarrier behind his own goal line
Secondary Receiver: A pass receiver who is not the primary target of the passer
Screen Block: When an offensive player attempts to station himself between the defensive player and the ballcarrier
Screen Pass: An offensive play in which the defensive rushers are allowed to penetrate before a short pass is thrown to a receiver behind a wall of blockers
Secondary: The area of the field guarded by defensive backs
Shiver: A blow usually delivered by a lineman in which he uses his forearm or open hand
Sidelines: The football field's side boundaries

Split End: A wide receiver who lines up at least 10 yards to the outside of the nearest offensive lineman

Sweep: An end run in which the runner has the help of several blockers in front of him

Swing: A pass pattern in which one of the backs loops around one flank of the backfield and catches the ball behind the line of scrimmage

T-Formation: A popular offensive alignment in which the backfield forms a T with the three running backs in a straight line behind the quarterback and parallel to their own line

Tackle: A line position outside the guard position. Also the act of stopping the ballcarrier.

Touchdown: When a player carries the football across his opponent's goal line, catches a pass in his opponent's end zone, or recovers a fumble and his team is awarded six points

Turnover: When the defense gets possession of the ball due to a fumble by the offense or an interception

Wide Receiver: A player eligible to catch a pass who is stationed on a flank when the play starts

Zone Defense: A defensive coverage in which players guard a specific area of the field instead of specific players